What's it like
BEING YOU?

OTHER BOOKS BY JOHN-ROGER

Blessings Of Light

Divine Essence

Dream Voyages

Forgiveness–The Key
To The Kingdom

God Is Your Partner

Inner Worlds of Meditation

Journey of a Soul

Loving Each Day

Loving Each Day
for Moms and Dads

Loving Each Day for Peacemakers

Manual On Using the Light

Passage Into Spirit

Psychic Protection

Relationships:
Love, Marriage and Spirit

Sex, Spirit and You

Spiritual High

Spiritual Warrior:
The Art of Spiritual Living

The Consciousness of Soul

The Path To Mastership

The Power Within You

The Spiritual Family

The Spiritual Promise

Walking With The Lord

The Way Out Book

Wealth and Higher Consciousness

When Are You Coming Home?

OTHER BOOKS BY JOHN-ROGER & PAUL KAYE

Momentum: Letting Love Lead

Mandeville Press, P.O. Box 513935, Los Angeles, CA 90051-1935

jrbooks@mandevillepress.org

www.mandevillepress.org

What's it like BEING YOU?

living life as your true self

JOHN-ROGER, D.S.S.
with PAUL KAYE, D.S.S.

Mandeville Press
Los Angeles, California

Mandeville Press
P.O. Box 513935
Los Angeles, CA 90051-1935
323-737-4055
jrbooks@mandevillepress.org
www.mandevillepress.org

Printed in the United States of America
ISBN 1-893020-25-8

Take someone who doesn't keep score,
Who's not looking to be richer, or afraid of losing,
Who has not even the slightest interest in his own
personality:
He's free.

Rumi

Life is performance art,
and the ultimate performance
is to play yourself.

Paul Kaye

Talk yourself into being in Soul.
Fantasize about being who you are.
Once you are in that fantasy, it becomes authentic.

I know that in my Soul I am free.
If you don't know how to do that, pretend you do.

John-Roger

You are not your bank account, or your ambitiousness.
You're not the cold clay lump with a big belly you leave
behind when you die.

You're not your collection of walking personality disorders.
You are spirit, you are love.

Anne Lamott

it takes courage to grow up
and turn out to be
who you really are

ee cummings

ACKNOWLEDGMENTS

Putting together a book is a team effort. We would like to thank Joan Oliver for the grace and ease with which she handled the Herculean task of editing the material, Vincent Dupont for catching the vision and gently guiding the project from its inception to completion, Stephen Keel for his refined understanding and meticulousness, Betsy Alexander for her wise counsel, Shelley Noble for her always superb and creative designing skills, David Sand for his keen eye and advice, Laren Bright for being there when we need him, and Howard Lawrence for his assistance and contribution. A special thanks to John Morton for his steady, loving commitment and support.

FOREWORD

It was a delightful honor to be invited to write the foreword to this valuable new book. I have always felt a deep resonance with John-Roger's work, which has flowed along pathways kindred to my own over the past decades. He has always spoken to me on the spiritual and the practical level in his writings, and this new work, written with Paul Kaye, is a sound example of the deep integration of practical spirituality that comes through in all his books.

What's It Like Being You? addresses one of the most important and profound subjects in the whole of human experience. At the heart of the book is the lifelong quest for authenticity. Many of us spend the first part of our lives acquiring layer after layer of false selves designed to get recognition, avoid pain, and navigate the often rocky territory of parental interactions. Later, in our schooling, we add more layers to get the approval of teachers, get our peers to like us, and find our way up the slippery slope to adulthood. Then, in adult life, we discover that the very false selves that helped us survive childhood stand between us and what it takes to lead a successful adult life. As one of my students put it, "I spent the first thirty years of my life pretending to be somebody else, and the next thirty years trying to find the real me underneath it all." If we succeed at this quest we get to enjoy the precious treasures available in what I call The Cathedral of the Real. We get to know our true feelings and to understand our true needs. We get to see the genius of our minds at work when we are free from the cloud cover of illusion. We can feel our organic spiritual nature as we become liberated from the grip of dogma.

In this quest for our essential wholeness we now have a road map and guidebook to the journey: *What's It Like Being You?* In it you will find the journey described in a way that is immensely practical and expansively spiritual. Your steps along the way will be guided by the time-tested wisdom that can only be gained by mindful, heartful personal experience.

In book after book, I have come to think of John-Roger as a veritable fountain of wisdom. The present volume, written with co-author Paul Kaye, shows that this tradition of nourishing practical knowledge continues with gusto.

If you are a seeker of deep communion with your true self, step through the gateway this book provides into the vastness of the universe it embraces. You will be in good company indeed.

GAY HENDRICKS, PH.D.
Bestselling author of *Conscious Living*,
and founder of The Hendricks Institute

You can't help but be who you are:

that's what breathes you.

Your problems come

when you pretend

to be someone else.

INTRODUCTION

We all play many parts in life: daughter or son, sister or brother, parent, boss, employee, leader, assistant, friend. We also play many different characters, sometimes in a single day: we can be a hero at work and an average Joe at home, or vice versa. But what if beyond all those parts and characters, there is a more fundamental role you can play—your true self, the you who is uniquely you? What if you were so familiar with this role that you were completely comfortable with yourself and at ease in all circumstances?

There's a wonderful story about a rabbi who dies and goes to heaven. He has led a devoted life, following as closely as he could in the footsteps of the prophets and sages, and so, naturally, he expects God to greet him with praise. But when the rabbi arrives at the pearly gates, God just looks at him and says, "I made you uniquely you. Why did you spend your life trying to be someone else?"

This book is a guide to being yourself. The reflections, practices, and inspirational quotations are designed to assist you in becoming who you really are. Only you can answer the question posed in the title: *What's it like being you?* But in these pages, you can explore a variety of approaches to help you connect with your true self.

First and foremost, this book is practical, aimed at giving you the *experience* of living in your true self as both a spiritual practice and an antidote to the stress of modern life. We now have conclusive evidence that stress has serious health consequences, weakening the immune system, damaging the heart, and affecting memory cells in the brain—just for starters. In a recent *New York Times* article, neuroscientist Bruce S. McEwen of Rockefeller University pointed out:

> We're now living in a world where our systems are not allowed a chance to rest, to go back to base line. They're being driven by excess calories, by inadequate sleep, by lack of exercise, by smoking, by isolation, or frenzied competition.

But there is truly no rush to go anywhere. Nobody is leaving this earth alive. The true self waits patiently for us to come to it. So why not slow down and enjoy the path of self-discovery?

Lao Tsu, the ancient Chinese philosopher, said: "In the pursuit of learning, every day something is acquired, and in the pursuit of spirit, every day something is dropped." It is my hope that in addition to gaining something from reading this book, you will also come away feeling lighter and freer from having let something go. The false self (everything that is not truly you) is what you surrender in the process of becoming who you are. When you strip away the opinions and postures and addictions of the ego-driven personality, what remains is the role of a lifetime—playing yourself. You can start anytime. Why not right now? As you move away from the self-defeating patterns of the false self, you move closer to the source of nourishment and renewal. Here in the true self— the Soul—we find Spirit, and we come alive.

Please Note:

The following words are used interchangeably throughout the book:

- False self, personality, ego
- True self, Soul
- God, Spirit

The John-Roger quotations on the left-hand pages are designed to assist you in attuning to the true self.

The Soul has no concern about time or space.
In the midst of personal travails, the Soul is laughing.
When you are concerned that someone
doesn't love you or might reject you or that you'll be fired,
the Soul is saying,
"Wow! New excitement, new adventure!"
You're afraid you'll starve, and the Soul is saying,
"This is wonderful; we might lose some weight."
You're distraught that you might not
be able to make your car payments,
and the Soul is saying, "We'll ride a bicycle or walk,
and get to see things at a more peaceful pace."
You think this is an idiotic philosophy,
but the Soul says, "This is the divine.'"

1

WHO ARE YOU?

Socrates said, "Know thyself." In Shakespeare's *Hamlet*, Polonius cautions, "To thine own self be true." But which self are we getting to know? To what self should we be true? Where is the self located anyway? Come to think of it, which self is reading these words?

These are questions that playwrights, philosophers, and other serious thinkers have been pondering since time immemorial. If the answers could be worked out through mathematical calculations or experimental measures, mathematicians and scientists would be the most enlightened people on the planet. But the self continues to elude even the greatest thinkers of our age.

We cannot reduce it to a formula, view it with high-tech, brain-imaging machinery, or define it conclusively in words. The self can only be lived and experienced from within. When we ask the age-old questions *Who am I?* and *Why am I here?*, we are joining thousands of generations of seekers who have set out to solve the mystery of incarnation, the riddle of human existence.

The nature of the Soul is joyful.
To participate consciously in Soul awareness,
you must come into harmony with its joyful nature.
Cultivate joyfulness in yourself and everything you do.
Joyfulness is more real than your problems.

Where we differ from those who have gone before us is not in the questions we ask but in the way we ask them. In less than a century, our world has changed so radically that we no longer have the appetite or opportunity for contemplation that our ancestors enjoyed. We seem to have lost the ability to slow down, to take time for ourselves. That's no surprise, for we are more rushed than ever. We have more information coming at us and less time to absorb it, as well as a lot more to do. Our continually rising expectations of what our lives should be like ensure that our days are overflowing with activity. The more conveniences we have, the more time we spend using and maintaining them. The more choices we have, the less we have to choose. Years ago, when there were just four television channels in the United States, it took only a moment to see that there was nothing we wanted to watch. Now, we have several hundred channels, and it can take us an hour to find out that there is nothing that really holds our interest.

Today our lives are filled with so many alternatives and oftentimes competing options that although the idea of simplifying our lives may sound like a good idea in theory, in reality it is nearly impossible to do. Yes, it's nice to stop and smell the roses, but then we have to add "shop for roses" to our to-do list. It's small wonder that a grassroots effort called the Slow Food Movement is spreading worldwide, as more and more of us look for ways to get back to what really matters. Carlo Petrini, the movement's founder, has this to say about what we face today:

> *If I live with the anxiety to go fast, I will not live*
> *well. My addiction to speed will make me sick. The*

The Soul, which is your greatest reality, is perfect.
You are already perfect in who you are and what you are.

art of living is to give time to each and every thing...Ultimately, "slow" means to take time to reflect. It means to take time to think. With calm, you arrive everywhere.

The ability to engage in self-reflection is uniquely human. If we lose that, do we lose our humanity? A few years ago, there was a movie, *AI* (short for "artificial intelligence"), about a highly intelligent robotic youth. When the robot realizes that he isn't human, he develops a deep and unrelenting yearning to become a flesh-and-blood boy. We tend to take our human experience for granted. An essential part of being human is having a physical body. The robot in *AI* had a physical body, albeit a mechanical one, but he lacked the crucial animating factor—the capacity for thought, emotion, and imagination.

Imagination is the source of creativity and innovation. With imagination comes choice: we can imagine negativity and harm, or what is helpful and positive. We can even use imagination to assist in our own healing: science has demonstrated that our mental imagery can change the way the brain and other body systems function.

Human beings also have emotions. We can love, hate, feel fear or joy. Sometimes we don't feel good, but at least we're feeling, something that's impossible for a robot. Emotions give dimension and color to the human experience.

You don't have to be all things to all people.

Don't even try to. Just be you, to you.

That is one of the great challenges.

Unlike robots, we have a mind that can reason, solve problems, and direct our energy, as well as self-reflect. We are free to point our minds in a positive or a negative direction.

We also have an unconscious, a vast repository of repressed and disowned thoughts, feelings, wishes, and dreams, along with unresolved and uncompleted experiences. Even when this unconscious material does not surface into awareness, it can strongly influence our conscious thoughts, feelings, and behavior.

In short, the human experience is so vast, so layered, so multidimensional that it is unlikely science could ever design a robot approaching such complexity. What is even more miraculous is that all the ingredients of our humanity comprise only a small part of the rich experience available to us as *total beings.*

This total being is the true self, who we really are. Who we *think* we are, or want others to think we are, is the false self.

THE FALSE SELF

There are many aspects to the false self, qualities you will no doubt recognize. I've listed the most familiar ones below; I'm sure you could come up with more:

Self-delusion
Anxiety/Worry
Judgment
Pretense

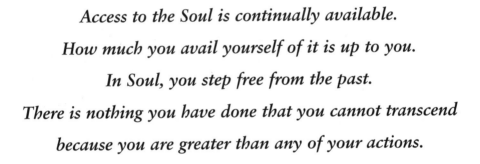

Access to the Soul is continually available.
How much you avail yourself of it is up to you.
In Soul, you step free from the past.
There is nothing you have done that you cannot transcend
because you are greater than any of your actions.

Anger
Fear
Need for Control

"Need for control" is probably the most prominent characteristic of the false self. It is from this that many other characteristics spring. Often the need for control runs our lives, which is ironic considering that, in reality, we have very little control over what happens in the world around us. Thus, the path of control is a futile one, inevitably leading to frustration and disappointment.

The false self's characteristic need for control sends it on a search for power from external sources. We have to seek outside ourselves for something to make us feel good. We are constantly looking for that event, that nod of approval, that recognition that will make us feel more secure. This constant search for approval is evidence of the false self's insatiable need for recognition by any means, even negative ones.

The false self is also called the personality or ego. Some aspects of it are inherited; others are developed through our experiences with family, friends, the culture we live in, our education, and our religious upbringing. Though aspects of the personality may change over the lifetime, the false self tends to become frozen and rigid, full of regret and resentment over missed opportunities. Even when the false self is able to break out of its rut, it usually jumps into another one. A new marriage may repeat the same patterns that doomed the previous one. Giving up smoking often leads to overeating. Is there a way out? Yes, but not through the

Not a single moment goes by
that does not bring you the opportunity
to know the Soul more deeply and more fully.
You are the vehicle for experiencing
and knowing your Soul.
So relax, hold back nothing, and let your Soul be.
When you make space for the blessings of Soul to manifest,
you become a living blessing.

false self. When we live in the false self, our lives are narrow, confined, and repetitious, although it may take us years to see that pattern emerge. Life is so diverse and diverting that it continually offers "just one more" thing that promises to fulfill us.

Another notable characteristic of the false self is its tendency to judge. Much as we may hate to admit it, judging others feels good, in the short term at least. It gives us a momentary sense of superiority and strength.

We also use judgment to put ourselves down. We may spend an unnecessary amount of time comparing ourselves to others, and when we find that they have things (or qualities) we don't have, we beat ourselves up. We may tell ourselves we need to improve, which sounds very well-intentioned, but it is really a subtle form of self-judgment. It just may be that you're perfect the way you are. Rather than feeling inadequate when you see that someone else has more worldly success than you, ask yourself why you can't accept yourself the way you are.

Often, instead of accepting ourselves as we are, we judge ourselves and seek to change. Getting us to change is what advertising is all about. If you watch TV these days you can't help noticing the pharmaceutical industry's ads. Even when you don't have a certain medical condition, all you have to do is sit through one of those commercials and you'll find yourself imagining you have a full-blown case.

At the same time that we want to know

who we are and that we are Soul,

we can so easily get stuck in the drama of daily living.

We become attached to our mistakes and failures

instead of learning how to experience success

beyond our wildest dreams.

A key to expansion,

to opening sacred inner space,

is the divine imagination.

Visualize the very best of yourself—

the joy and the loving flowing within you and out of you—

and hold that vision.

As you hold that vision,

it will become a reality

because that's the real you.

Say you're watching a *Seinfeld* rerun, and during one commercial break, there's an ad that asks, "Have you ever been anxious?" You find yourself nodding. "Have you ever been worried?" Another nod. "Do you have a strong urge to go shopping?" Now you're holding your head in your hands, saying "Oh, yes, that's me. I'm a mess." The ad goes on to tell you that you have *psychodyslexaphobia*. Just ask your doctor to prescribe Anysyndrome for you. The spokesperson then lists—very rapidly—the drug's side effects: headache, dry mouth, muscle pain, severe diarrhea...and impotence! If you haven't already tuned out, you think, "Hey, it's worth whatever it takes not to have that problem again."

Instant cures are very appealing: life today is so busy and complex that we'll do anything to solve our problems as quickly as possible. But I see it differently. Life is not a problem to be solved. It's a journey of awakening, and that journey is not a race. You can run, walk, or crawl to enlightenment; the pace is up to you. But trying to change the false self by judging it is doomed to fail, because judgment itself is a product of the false self. You'd simply be going around in circles.

As Einstein pointed out, you can't solve a problem with the same consciousness that caused it. The false self seduces us into thinking it can cleanse itself of negativity. For example, we may judge ourselves for overeating or overspending, and then get angry with ourselves in the name of purging our perceived inadequacies. Yet we continue to overeat and overspend. This is the human

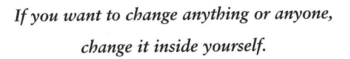

If you want to change anything or anyone,

change it inside yourself.

dilemma: even when we want to break an attachment to self-defeating behavior, we don't; we merely exchange one false-self pattern for another.

The fifteenth-century Indian mystical poet Kabir expressed this paradox wonderfully:

> *I gave up sewn clothes, and wore a robe,*
> *but I noticed one day the cloth was well woven.*
>
> *So I bought some burlap, but I still*
> *throw it elegantly over my left shoulder.*
>
> *I pulled back my sexual longings,*
> *and now I discover that I'm angry a lot.*
>
> *I gave up rage, and now I notice*
> *that I am greedy all day.*
>
> *I worked hard at dissolving the greed,*
> *And now I am proud of myself.*

False-self behavior can keep us busy for a lifetime while nothing really changes. We don't *have* to change anything. But we may *want* to change our perspective, our outlook on life. The false self functions in the realm of personality, the ego. In this realm we identify with what we look like, what we do, how much money we have. But what would happen if we shifted our perspective? Instead of seeing ourselves as stressed-out human beings grasping for enlightenment, for some kind of spiritual experience, what if we realized that we are spiritual beings having a human experience? That spiritual being is the true self.

I'm asking that you go to the place

that responds when you hold a child,

the place that awakens when you help someone

just for the pleasure of doing it.

Connect with the sacred energy

that comes alive when you express loving.

THE TRUE SELF

If we see ourselves as having any spiritual component at all, we might think that the split is at best fifty-fifty between personality and Soul. But, in reality, it's more like ninety-ten in favor of the spiritual side, the true self. The true self is like the sun: it's much bigger and brighter than the false self, which, like the moon, generates no light in itself and shines only as a reflection of the sun.

So what exactly is this true self that shines so brightly, and how do we get in touch with it? Often, it is easier for us to recognize the true self in others than in ourselves. Think of a person who seems to radiate something special. What is that quality? As children, most of us had someone in our lives—a relative, perhaps, or a neighbor or a teacher or a local shopkeeper—who always had a smile for us and a twinkle in their eye. Without knowing why, we were drawn to that person. He or she might have had a hard and difficult life but somehow had managed to avoid judgment, bitterness, and cynicism—had managed to transcend the human condition, in other words, and live from the center we call the Soul, the true self.

Here are some of the qualities of the true self:

Loving (the action of love)
Cooperation
Spiritual Essence
Joyfulness
Enthusiasm

Long ago,

I told myself that whenever a feeling

of depression came over me,

it would immediately move me to joy.

In other words,

I reprogrammed depression for happiness.

Anything less than a state of loving

can be used to reprogram you back into a state of loving.

Anything off-center

can be used to move you back to center.

Acceptance
Peace

If, indeed, we are spiritual beings, then why, when the false self is running around screaming and beating itself up, doesn't the true self do something to stop it? Perhaps the true self is waiting for us to be quiet and pay attention to it for a few moments, so that it can impart its wisdom and love. To connect with the true self, we need to leave the behavioral field of the false self and enter the field of the true self.

One way we can enter the field of the true self is through observation. We all have an inner observer that watches us as we play out our human experience in the world. This inner observer is aware of the body and its movement. It notices when we are lost in fantasy or when we feel depressed. It watches our minds drive us crazy with racing thoughts and nonstop chatter. When you ask the question, "Who am I?" it is the observer who knows. This awareness is present and alert at all times, monitoring the body, mind, emotions, and imagination. The observer is nonjudgmental, neutral, and unconditionally loving. This is the true self.

The true self has its own language. Joyfulness and loving—love in action—are expressions of the true self. This form of loving is not to be confused with romantic love. Romantic love is conditional: we love someone for what they will do for us or give us, and once they stop giving us what we want, we withdraw our love and give it to someone else we think will fill our needs. The loving expression of the true self is giving, free, and unconditional.

It's important to maintain our optimism
so that we will find what is always present inside us.
When we find it, it is not an end,
signaled with a bell or a round of applause;
it is a new beginning, and it is ongoing.
Soul is here, now.

When loving is unconditional, it is not dependent on how others behave. We will continue to love someone regardless of what they do or say. We may not condone their behavior, and we may choose not to be with them, but our love for them is not conditioned in any way. Unconditional love is like that of a mother for her child. No matter what the child does—poops, cries, poops again—the mother's loving remains constant, a consistent and nonjudging presence.

Unconditional loving as the nature of the true self is beautifully described in a poem by Antonio Machado:

> *I dreamt...*
> *that I had a beehive*
> *here inside my heart.*
> *And the golden bees*
> *were making white combs*
> *and sweet honey*
> *from my old failures.*

Perhaps the best way to move out of the false self and into the true self is to use the most powerful tool at our disposal: unconditional loving. As you review the list of false-self attributes on page 11, check the ones you identify with and add your own if they are not on the list. Say that the attributes on your list are uptight, pretending, anxious, judging, worrying, egotistical; then you would say to yourself:

> *I love myself even though I feel uptight. I love myself even when I am pretending to be something I am not. I love*

One way you can learn
to maintain the Soul center,
which is oneness with God,
is to bring together all aspects
of your life's expression
in the attitude of loving.

*myself in those times when I feel anxious. I love myself
even though I am judging. I love myself when I worry. I
love myself even when I am being egotistical.*

In other words, don't let anything you do—no matter how wrong
or petty or shameful it seems—stand in the way of your loving. Let
your loving embrace every part of you, because that loving, and
the joyfulness that comes with it, is truly who you are.
Unconditional acceptance is the way to deal with the false self so
that we may live in our spiritual nature.

There is a simple but powerful exercise you can use in any
situation to move out of the false self and into the true self. Say
you are driving and someone cuts in front of you, or you are stuck
in traffic when you have an important appointment to get to, or
you're in a hurry to go somewhere and the kids are screaming, or
your boss is really on your case, or you're calling your health
insurer and get stuck in an automated-phone-system nightmare,
whatever the situation, just say three words: **I love this.** Repeat this
phrase in a neutral way, whether you mean it or not. This can be
said silently or aloud.

The outward situation may not change—at least not right away—
though you may smile or relax a little. More important, in
repeating those words you momentarily leave the field of the false
self, where well-being is conditional, and put yourself in the energy
of love. When you say, "I love this," you are taking a big step
toward accessing the infinite reservoir of unconditional love that
your true self possesses and that is always available to you.

God continually breathes toward you

the wind that blows from heaven.

As you open yourself to let it in,

you'll find that you can't hold on to it,

you can't possess it.

You must let go and allow that wind to lift you until you

manifest your true self,

the beingness of your Soul.

Then you will know yourself as divine,

as the promised one,

as the Beloved for whom you have searched.

And you will be awakened to the Soul

and will know the presence of God in your heart.

Another way to attune yourself to the true self is to give your full attention to the rising and falling of your breath. As you observe your breath in a neutral and loving way, ask yourself, *What is it that is observing the breath?* In simply observing the breath, we move further and further into the field of the true self. And as we do, we feel more joyful, more enthusiastic, and more naturally loving about the human experience, no matter how crazy it seems at times.

Whenever you want to call on God,
all you need to do is sit quietly and listen.
If nothing happens and all you experience is stillness,
that's wonderful, too. God is in that stillness.

SILENCE

This book is about how to live as the true self—how to exist at the calm center of creation, instead of in the ego-personality. Habitually, we live on the periphery, buffeted this way and that by someone else's opinion of us or by comparing ourselves with others and coming up short. We may be so anxious to get to our Soul center that we try to take a shortcut through another person's personality, adopting their laugh, their smile, their walk, their ideas until we're totally lost. When we start to wonder, "Who am I?" it's time to turn to the silence within. In that silence, we listen.

When we center ourselves in silence, we make the choice to become open and willing to live life fully. Regardless of what comes to us, we become willing to expand instead of pulling back—contracting—when we don't like what's happening. Expansion is the key. In response to negative feelings, we become more spacious inside, embracing the bad as well as the good. When we accept ourselves fully as we are, we no longer strive against our own true nature.

Whenever you find that you are out of touch with your loving, simply move into the quiet center within. Let go of any expectation that something has to happen. When you are free of any pressure to perform that you have placed on yourself, and you

The Soul will not entertain you.

It's not its job to create psychic phenomena.

Your job is to sit in silence and be open to the Soul

and start the process of awakening to your knowing.

As you awaken, the Soul can replace the ego and

personality as the center of consciousness and energy,

though it still uses the vehicles of the mind,

the emotions, the imagination, and the body

to function in the world.

become still, love arises naturally. Sometimes it's when you do nothing that the loving appears in its clearest form.

As you go into the silence within, bypassing the body, emotions, mind, and unconscious, you connect with the energy that is your Soul, and start to contain it. In silence the energy of your Soul builds. You naturally empower yourself by going inward and becoming very, very quiet.

For this practice, find a quiet place where you won't be disturbed. As you go into the quiet, inevitably the mind will kick in. You may find yourself having conversations with your boss, planning the weekend with your kids, or going over your shopping list. There is no need to resist this or see it as a bad thing. Have a piece of paper and a pen near you and jot down what is useful. Perhaps the silence is letting you know something. Maybe you really need that item at the supermarket. Write it down and return to the silence. (When you return to your daily activities, it's a good idea to follow up on what you wrote down so you can have completion and build trust with yourself.)

Giving your boss a piece of your mind, while you are connecting with the silence, is probably not very useful. So you can let that go. You may have to search out the silence and the stillness within you. It's like going on an adventure. Make up your own movie, for example, *In Search of the Silence*. You may find your mind taking you to the beach where you are riding a horse at low tide. Part of the adventure is to find the silence while you are on that fantasy

Someone looking from the outside

might not notice the difference in you,

which can be a real slap to the ego,

so the ego may want to reassert itself,

out of self-importance.

But if you are in your ego, you are not in your Soul.

You will know you are in your Soul

when you are just being ordinary,

just living your life simply and directly,

doing what is in front of you

without looking for recognition.

ride. In other words, whatever the mind produces, attempt to find the silence within it.

It's easy to fall into the trap of waiting for things in your life to be perfect so that you can then find the silence and stillness within you. And, of course, it's nice to go on retreat or on a mountain and sit in a quiet environment, but that in no way means your mind will leave you alone. Besides, most of us don't have that luxury, so we might as well get on with finding the silence right now. It is one of the most valuable things you can do for yourself. You'll relax, have greater clarity, and touch in to your true self.

Stay clear of anything that suggests to you,

"I can't seek God until I have a wife,

until I have a husband, until I have kids,

until my kids grow up, until my next lifetime,

until I'm a different person," and so on.

God is for each one of us just as we are now.

If anything outside yourself becomes so vital to you

that acquiring it is more important than peace of mind

and tranquility of Soul, you are lost.

2

THE MANY PERFORMANCES OF YOU

We're stuck in the human condition, but instead of judging our stuckness, we can have fun with it. What if we looked at the whole human experience as an act, one we're very good at? Instead of bemoaning it, we could celebrate it. In Hollywood they give out Oscars for great film performances. Why shouldn't we get an award for our performance here on Earth?

Let's say you're nominated for best performance as a worrier. The other nominees include your mother (and her father, posthumously). You, however, have so perfected worrying that you are the overwhelming choice. Now what happens? Well, you've watched the Oscars and the Emmys and the Golden Globes. After you're announced as the winner, people stand up and applaud and cheer. You look appropriately shocked (even though you were pretty sure you would win and, true to character, have been worrying about your speech for weeks). You kiss the people sitting around you. The music is playing. The camera follows you on stage.

Living life is like looking in a mirror.

What is reflected back to us,

by way of other people,

is the state of our being, our consciousness.

If we are angry,

we may think that person over there is pretty angry.

If we're full of doubt,

then we may think that the other person is full of doubt.

The big secret is that beyond the mirror is the land of Soul.

You receive the award. More kisses. Then you blame—I mean, thank—your mother and father for a lifetime of guilt and the training they gave you and the genes that allowed you to play the role of worrier day after day, year after year. You thank your friends and family for all the support they have given you in worrying and for all their judgments about what is lacking in your life. And then the music starts playing, so you hold your award high, mention your spouse with tears in your eyes (even though you are separating) and blow everyone a kiss as you walk off stage.

We live in a culture that worships celebrity, and people pretend to be all sorts of things. The true self doesn't need fame or recognition or approval. But the false self is like a celebrity who needs a lot of attention and who screams and shouts until he gets it.

There's a story I like about Alexander the Great going to see the famous Greek philosopher Diogenes. Diogenes asks Alexander,

> *"What are you doing?"*
> *Alexander replies, "I'm going to conquer Greece."*
> *Diogenes asks, "And what are you going to do after that?"*
> *Alexander tells him, "I'm going to conquer Asia Minor."*
> *"And then what are you going to do?" Diogenes asks.*
> *"Then I'm going to conquer the world," Alexander replies.*
> *Again, Diogenes asks, "And after that what are you going to do?"*
> *"Then," says Alexander, very pleased with himself, "I'm going to relax and enjoy my life."*

Many people, when they hear about

using the divine imagination to live in the true self,

say, "But that's not real."

My response is, "Really?

You are divine.

You are a creator.

You have the essence of God manifesting through you.

Why can't you mock up something positive?

You mock up your misery.

You mock up your despair.

You mock up your illness.

Why not mock up who you are?"

You can use exactly the same principle

you use to put down yourself and others

to lift yourself into who you are.

Diogenes looks at Alexander for a long time and then
finally says, "You know, I can save you a lot of trouble.
Why don't you relax and enjoy it now?"

We often say to ourselves, "After I'm successful I'll be able
to do this, and then I'll do this, then this..." Yet all the time
we already have what we want inside of us. How ironic.
Outside, where we *think* the answers lie, there will always be more
we want, no matter how much we have. Inside, we are wealthy
beyond measure, and there is nothing stopping us from taking
full advantage of our treasure except our minds, which always
want to play an outer game. To win the outer game, certain things
have to happen: getting that job, receiving that raise, winning
that contract, getting married, conquering Mesopotamia.
Our satisfaction depends on circumstances. But the inner life
of loving, joy, and relaxation can be fulfilling regardless
of circumstances.

Can we "pretend" to be who we are, with honesty and integrity?
We know that we can change the body through training, the
imagination through creativity, the emotions through experience,
and the mind through learning. All these help us shape a new
self. But which self are we shaping? Is it a false self or an authentic
one? There are criteria we can use to find out. We know when
we are living in the authentic self when we are more loving and
caring toward ourselves and others, when we are not hurting
ourselves or others, when we appreciate and care for whatever
is in our lives, and when we can be of service without looking for
a reward.

Why do you need recognition?

You say, "I just feel like I need it."

Sacrifice your feelings.

You say, "I think I really need recognition."

Sacrifice your mind.

You say, "I need it."

That's ego. Sacrifice your ego.

What's left? Nothing.

That "nothing" is exactly what you are, here on the planet.

All the games you play are an attempt to

make yourself something you're not.

What you are is no-thing,

and no-thing is the very essence of God,

the Soul, present here and now.

Most of us live in the false self 99 percent of the time. We are concerned with image—how we come across to others—and with being successful (which, in this culture, usually means having a lot of money). But no matter how much money and success the false self acquires, it is never enough, so we remain greedy for more. We compare ourselves to others and come up short; then we collapse in feelings of lack and fear about the future. It is a vicious circle: each fix, each solution, becomes tomorrow's problem.

And yet the true self is always present, silent in the midst of all of the commotion, remaining loving, joyful, and unconditional. Since the false self is just an act, whatever we do as the false self— worrying, being impatient, judging—is merely a performance. We watch movies to distract us, seek professional help to counsel us, turn to the pharmaceutical industry to drug us, and look to religion to inspire us. We go on weight-loss diets and mental diets; we meditate and go on retreat. And still we are discontented.

In all these efforts at self-improvement, we miss the truth: life is as simple as breathing in and breathing out. Most of what we struggle with is what we've added on to that simple action: our expectations, desires, fears, insecurities, and projections. If we are going to find any peace, we need to take responsibility for our part in shaping our lives. And our part is everything. We are responsible for it all—the good, the bad, the ugly. We either created it or promoted it or allowed it. We will struggle a lot less if, whatever happens, we say, "I love this," and return to the simplicity of breathing in and breathing out. No matter what we

Remember that this world is the land of illusion.
There is much that goes on here that is not real
and only appears to be real when it is experienced
through the mind, emotions, or imagination.
When you can observe directly from the reality of the Soul,
the threat in most situations disappears,
and you realize that there is nothing here to hurt you.
You hurt yourself when you
misidentify the situation at hand.

think, the world is perfect the way it is. Our problem is that we don't always like it that way.

All around us, however, we can see people who have managed to find a blessing in the midst of tragedy. If you can take just one day and live it with full awareness that you are completely responsible for whatever happens, and if you can observe yourself neutrally and lovingly in the process, you will be transformed. You will see everything as perfect, and will realize that life really is as simple as breathing in and breathing out.

Come back to your day-to-day life. In watching your own performance, you may see that it's not worry you excel at but unworthiness or anger or any of the other false-self attributes. Take a moment to recall two or three of your most famous and oft-repeated lines: "I can't have a good time or relax unless I'm rich." "It's all hopeless, so I might as well give up." "I'm not worthy, and it's all my parents' fault."

As you repeat these lines, you'll realize that, like any actor, you're reading from a script. Ask yourself this:

Whose script am I reading? Who wrote these lines?

You'll probably find that your lines come from a specific individual or from a combination of influential people in your life. You can certainly add to that anything you picked up from a character you admired in a television show, movie, or book. Then you filled in the rest. Isn't it interesting to discover that when we complain about life, we are reading a script of our own making?

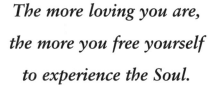

The more loving you are,

the more you free yourself

to experience the Soul.

But it's also important to be aware that your performance has been honed over time and has been supported by your environment and your own self-talk, what you have told yourself. Now it's time to talk differently to yourself. You need another script.

While you are writing a new script for yourself, be sure it includes new nonverbal cues. Scientists have discovered that our facial expressions not only speak volumes to others but also communicate important messages to our own hormones and immune system.

In addition to the script, any performance has another key component: the director. The second important question to ask yourself is this:

Who is directing my performance?

For some people, the answer will be clear: "my mother," or maybe "my dad." So not only are you reading your mother's or father's script, but your parent is directing you from the place within you where you have internalized their messages. Perhaps it is not clear who the director is. Regardless, the point of this question, like the previous one, is to give you pause, so that you will realize you are playing a part and consider whether you want to continue.

Perhaps your performance focuses on feeling that you are not getting what you want. Perhaps you like to act self-righteous and condescending. Maybe the script says that you think you will never have enough. But all the while you are performing, the true self is present and alive inside you—

When you seek love through sex
or an emotional attachment
or when you lust after a new car or new home,
you are really—deep inside yourself—
trying to locate your Soul.
You just go "way out" instead of "way in" to find it.
The loneliness that you feel is just loneliness
for your true self, your Soul.

loving, joyful, and accepting. The true self is allowing your performance to play itself out, perhaps for a lifetime, but at least until you start investigating what script you're reading from and who is directing you.

Most of us are tired of repeating the same lines over and over and of being directed into action that no longer works for us. Still, we typecast ourselves, assigning ourselves the same roles, repeating the same performances. Even when we think we're taking on a different part, it turns out to be the same old play. This is the way of the false self, the conditional way of life.

Fortunately, there is a way out. It is not through blaming others or feeling like a victim or judging. That traps us in the false self's field of behavior. The way out is through the true self, which is unconditional and unconditionally loving. When we approach life in this way, we are free to write the script and choose the director. We may just choose to play ourselves, who we really are.

The poet Derrick Walcott wrote in "Love After Love," "The time will come / when, with elation, / You will greet yourself arriving / At your own door…" When we arrive at our own door and the true self greets us, what is the script we've been living that got us to that place? To step into the role of the true self, we will need a different script from the one for our award-winning false-self role. More on this later.

The journey to the true self will take you through your body, imagination, emotions, mind, and unconscious because these are

The Soul is not something apart from you,

held in reserve for later.

The Soul is entirely present with you

every moment of the day and night.

It is the dynamic part of you that is ever present.

It is you, not the fictional you, but the real you.

As you discern its reality more and

allow it to express itself,

you will find your life becoming lighter and freer,

more joyful and more fun.

You can have all of that right now.

the conditions of the human experience. Take a moment now to observe yourself. You may feel out of balance, your mind may be jumping around, but you can still observe yourself. Your inner observer will not be waving a flag to get your attention, but if you are still and aware and present, you will sense its presence.

What if that which is aware—your inner observer—is *God?* How ironic to think that we are running around looking for Spirit, for God, and all the while God is inside us, looking at us looking for Him. A lot of us think that if God were present, there would be more going on, golden chariots or a choir of angels. We look for something phenomenal, something that will make us feel special. But maybe God is present in the ordinary act of observing.

The man whispered, "God, speak to me,"
and a meadowlark sang, but the man did not hear.
And the man yelled, "God, speak to me," and the thunder
and lightening lit the sky, but the man did not listen.
The man looked around and said, "God, let me see you,"
and a star shined brightly, but the man did not see.
And the man shouted, "God, show me a miracle,"
and a life was born, but the man did not notice.
So the man cried out in despair, "Touch me, God,
and let me know you are here."
Whereupon God reached down and touched the man,
but the man brushed the butterfly away and walked on.

—Anonymous

Soul awareness is easy to get into
and just as easy to fall out of.

We fall out of Soul awareness so easily
because the world wants us to go that way.
The material world has a billion distractions,
so you need to watch where you place your focus
and be careful what you create.

If you want Soul, find joy in yourself
and in everything around you.

The false self, however, doesn't want to give up being the center of our universe. It wants to engage us in a fight because that very act of taking a position, of opposing the false self, keeps the game going on *its* terms. But if, instead of fighting the false self, we love it without conditions, we enter the realm of the true self. Automatically, the game ends.

MY SELF OR NOT?

In getting to know ourselves, we must come to love ourselves—not just the part we consider positive, but all of it: good, bad, light, dark, our strengths as well as our weaknesses. In fact, self-acceptance is essential to our health.

The human immune system is designed, via chemical markers called antigens, to label cells "self" or "not self." Once a cell is labeled "not self"—foreign to the body—substances in the blood called antibodies attach themselves to the "not-self" cells and target them for destruction. In this way, the immune response saves your life.

There is an interesting counterpart in the psyche. When we disown part of ourselves through denial, self-judgment, or feeling victimized, we disempower ourselves emotionally and spiritually. Through our negative thoughts and emotions—directed back at ourselves—we actually attack and weaken the body and the immune system. Just as the immune system targets "non-self" cells for destruction, judging or disowning what we see as physical or personality flaws sends a message to our unconscious that this part

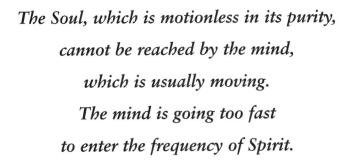

The Soul, which is motionless in its purity,

cannot be reached by the mind,

which is usually moving.

The mind is going too fast

to enter the frequency of Spirit.

of us is "not self" and, therefore, must be destroyed. In attacking our wholeness, we are rejecting the true self and giving ourselves over to the false self, which lives in anger, worry, and fear.

Instead, we must embrace all aspects of ourselves. The true self is divine, a Soul, part of God. We must own that we are spiritual beings with infinite abundance and authentic power. Anything less is denial of our true nature and inevitably leads to problems for us—physically, emotionally, and mentally.

There are diseases that result from the breakdown of the immune system. When the body is no longer able to recognize the chemical markers or antigens, it cannot activate the immune cells to destroy foreign invaders. The invaders then replicate unchecked, and the body moves into disease and, eventually, death.

The counterpart in the psyche relates to false loyalties: placing loyalty to our ego, or emotions, or beliefs above loyalty to the Soul. Not recognizing these fixations as impostors, as "not self," we give them space to reside inside us, where they proliferate. When we become attached to our illusions ("money is the answer to everything," is one example) and cannot let them go, we are making what is "not self"—the illusions—part of "self." Then these illusions, disguised as "self," begin to erode the very foundation of our worldview. As we reinforce our illusions, it becomes increasingly difficult to distinguish true from false. We cling to ideas that separate us from the true self. These positions aren't truly "ours" because they're not arising from the

The physical world is full of errors

and frustrations and mistakes.

They are all opportunities to refine your level

of awareness so you can get closer to who you are.

Who you are is so subtle that many of you have been

in your Soul and out the other side without realizing

it. The Soul is a small, integral unit of energy,

yet the cosmos and all the universes

are contained within it.

The Soul is the prototype for all existence.

It goes beyond the intellect.

true self. They're the vehicles through which the false self seeks to maintain control.

As we learn to discriminate between what is true for us and what is a product of someone else's belief system, we are no longer so loyal to our illusions. True to ourselves, we lead a healthier life physically, mentally, and emotionally.

Any negativity is just pointing out

the next thing for us to work on

and to bring across into the Divinity,

until one day, and truthfully so,

it will all be divine

and we will know it as that.

There will still be negativity,

and there will still be positivity,

and we will see it all equally as the Divine.

That is our heritage.

Practice

OBSERVE: IT'S ALL EQUAL

This practice asks you to take part of your day—I suggest 15 minutes to start—and simply observe yourself. Pay particular attention to the times you judge yourself or others. When you catch yourself judging others, inwardly say, "I am no more or less than anyone else. I love it all." When you realize you are judging yourself, inwardly say, "I forgive myself for judging myself."

Above all, practice being loyal to your Soul. You do that by loving yourself through all your experiences and realizing that there is no value in putting yourself down. There are far better choices to make, and the best one is to love it all.

When you are willing to own all of yourself, embracing the light and dark sides equally, you are better able to feel love and compassion for yourself and others. The true self experiences life with no split in consciousness, seeing everything as perfect, just as it is. This frees you to live life in a more integrated and spontaneous way.

It is important to understand
that you probably won't gain
an advantage over others
by having an open heart.
All that is going to happen
is that you will live in a
higher state of consciousness
while you walk through this world.
That's it. And that's enough.

3

HOW MANY YOUS ARE THERE?

We say we want to know ourselves, but when it comes to the actual process of putting our attention into self-knowledge and confronting our habits, we often run out of steam. Yet if it weren't possible to transform, I wouldn't be teaching how to do it. Inner growth and change are definitely possible; many have done it, and it doesn't require a big bank account, a long training course, or special equipment. It requires something much more valuable: consistent application.

I'm not suggesting that transformation is easy. Even the butterfly breaking from the cocoon struggles into its beauty. I don't look at struggle as a negative, however, but as a stretching and opening process.

The greatest ballet dancers in the world return to the barre every day, throughout their careers. They join all the other dancers in the troupe in the basic exercises. It's the same with the great basketball players, constantly practicing shooting hoops. Over and over, the

As a matter of fact, we're all ordinary,

which is the prior condition to God.

When we see ourselves as special,

we're actually moving further away from Spirit

than when we're just ordinary.

same moves. In the very ordinariness of that repetition lie the seeds of greatness.

The practice of being yourself is not drudgery. It's uplifting, it's a pleasure. But the people, places, and things of this world have such a pull that if we don't continually practice, we will be stuck in our false-self ways. The true self is the true God-force within you. It is important to practice placing your attention and your consciousness only with the true self.

One of the biggest challenges to living in the true self is keeping the focus on your own transformation, even when the people around you make it clear they wish you would revert to your old ways. But in the journey to the Soul, it is not so much others you need to cooperate with; it is the other selves inside of you.

You have already learned something about the false self and the true self. The true self, the Soul, enters the physical realm in order to know itself. Essentially, it is gaining experience. The Soul is pure and complete and a part of God, at the same time that it is on a journey of transcendence, to become one with God and experience its own fullness. The Soul's experiences here on Earth are its springboard to God's higher nature. In order to function on its earthly journey, the Soul has the assistance of what we call a conscious self, a high self, and a basic self.

The **CONSCIOUS SELF** is the self that is reading this book, the one you present to the world. A blank slate at birth, the conscious self

Go inside to your Soul.
Experience you as you,
so that there is no experience.
Then there is no separation—
no "he" and "me," no "she" and "me,"
no "God" and "me." There is only Oneness.
When this happens, life becomes a process
of simply moving through this world,
doing each thing that is presented to you.
You live in the protection of your Soul,
and an all-encompassing love becomes
almost tangible in the immediacy of its presence.

takes on the characteristics of the family, culture, and religion into which it is born and raised.

The HIGH SELF holds the blueprint of your life, with all the possibilities and permutations. You could think of the high self as a wise seer that makes sure you stay on track to accomplish what you have come into this world to learn. From a subtle-energy standpoint, we say that the high self resides outside your body, above the crown of your head.

The BASIC SELF keeps us on the physical plane and ensures that the body functions well, that the heart keeps beating, food is digested, and all the other physiological processes run smoothly. The basic self also oversees the functioning of energy centers of the body, known as chakras. The habits you establish are held in the basic self, which is located in the lower belly just below or just above the navel. Once a habit is established, the basic self seldom wants to let it go.

The three selves are intended to work as a harmonious team. The high self dishes out the life plan in manageable portions to the basic self. The basic self keeps the body going and provides the energy to move through the world. The conscious self steers the ship, providing clear direction. The design of the system is elegantly simple, but like most things of this world, it can go amiss.

You've no doubt seen a rebellious child whose parents have not provided clear boundaries and direction. The child yells and

If someone comes to you in anger,
respond in calmness;
it restores the balance within you.
If you feel resistance, manifest the opposite,
acceptance; this, too, restores the balance.

screams when it doesn't get what it wants, and it ends up controlling the parents in some ways. It's interesting to see the power a five-year-old can have over two adults. It's often the same with the basic self. Unless the conscious self provides good direction, the basic self can develop bad habits and start to steer the ship.

Scientists have recently discovered that the area in the abdomen where the basic self resides is so complex neurologically that it behaves like a second brain. You can make contact with the basic self simply by placing one hand on your abdomen just below your navel and the other hand just above it. Often, this will calm and relax you immediately.

Making physical contact with the basic self makes it easier to communicate with it. Say you had a hard day: someone was rude to you, or you argued with your boss. You can gently let the basic self know that all three selves did their best today and that the basic self did a very good job and can now let go of the incident. Perhaps you can forgive yourself for judging yourself if you did judge. If, after forgiving yourself, you spontaneously sigh or exhale deeply, that may be a sign that the basic self is letting go.

Another way for you, as the conscious self, to communicate with the basic self is to speak directly to it. In the morning, you can stand in front of a mirror, look into your eyes, in a relaxed way, and speak to your basic self, giving it clear, positive direction and encouragement for the day.

The very nature of the ego, its fundamental action,
is to withdraw, to isolate, and to separate itself.
It's the one who is self-obsessing and recoils
from every opportunity to move into Soul.
So if you ever say that you don't care about the Soul
or Spirit, you might want to consider
who inside of you is saying that.

To make any kind of lasting change in your thinking or behavior, it is essential to have the cooperation and support of your basic self. Without that cooperation, you will literally be fighting with yourself. Your old habits will reassert themselves as the basic self works to hold you in its comfort zone, which may contain myriad habit patterns, from overeating to procrastination.

The basic self often makes itself known through feelings of resistance. When you experience resistance to doing something you have decided is the best thing to do, take time to explain to your basic self why you are doing it and why you need the energy to take the action. It's important to be patient, clear, and loving with the basic self, just as you would with a child you were mentoring. To be sure you are making a responsible choice and to help get your basic self on board, you can ask yourself two questions:

If I choose to do this, what will be the effect of this choice on me?

If I choose to do this, what will be the effect of this choice on others?

Once you as a conscious self have chosen a direction and moved on it, and the basic self has been cooperative and supportive of what you are doing, it is time to reward it. You could go to a movie, read a good book, or allow yourself to sleep in one morning. You are rewarding the basic self for positive behavior (which, in turn, reinforces that behavior). One of our main problems, however, is that we tend to reward ourselves before we've completed—or even started—what we are trying to accomplish. Premature rewards send the wrong message to the

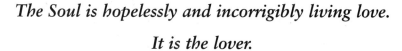

The Soul is hopelessly and incorrigibly living love.

It is the lover.

It goes on in blissful ignorance of

the pain and suffering experienced by

the personality, emotions, mind, and imagination.

The Soul relates to other Souls.

The rest is a game.

basic self. For example, if you reward yourself with ice cream before starting a project, you may set a bad precedent. Then, when you want to make a positive change, the basic self may resist: it has already had its reward, so why bother?

Building good habits can start at any time. It is important to keep the lines of communication open with your basic self. There may be times when you become very discouraged and despondent. Sometimes, when people are really feeling down, they say things like, "I just want to die." It's important to remember that the basic self is always awake and aware and very literal. If it hears a wish to die—even if you're just being melodramatic—it may take the words literally and begin to shut your body down. Given the growing body of scientific evidence showing that our thoughts can directly influence our physical health, it is essential to be very careful of the language you use. The messages you give yourself are critical to your well-being.

As you contemplate your new role in life, prepare to forgo worry and upset, and lead a more carefree existence, you will need to keep your basic self informed about what you're doing and why. Let it know you want its energy and support. Explain in a loving way how this new direction is going to be more fun and healthier for all three selves. Express clearly that the new direction is a reflection of the true self, which is natural and spontaneous and loving. Reassure the basic self that it will be part of that joy. Working with the basic self is a creative experience. Enjoy the process. You are building an essential, lifelong partnership.

You are loved just as you are right now.
Get that really clear in your heart.
There is nothing you have to do differently
to be loved by God.
Who you are is enough in itself.
This is the positive inner reality.
And it's the truth about you.
If the way you are and the way you behave
aren't joy-producing for you,
then you have the right and the ability to change.
Regardless, God's love is consistently available to you.

Practice

MEDITATION FOR ALIGNMENT WITH THE TRUE SELF

(CD included)

Inside the back cover of this book, you will find a CD with a 45-minute guided meditation designed to work specifically with the basic self. It will help the basic self, along with you, as a conscious self, to live in greater alignment with the true self. The high self is a neutral observer in this process.

The basic self manages our day-to-day affairs. It maintains the physical body and controls our instincts, memories, and habits. It is also the level through which we communicate with the high self and the high self communicates with us. The purpose of this guided meditation is to create a channel of communication between you, as a conscious self, and your basic self, so that you can transform negative or limiting habit patterns into more positive ones.

For best results, listen to the meditation at least once a day, for 33 *consecutive* days. There is no harm in listening to it more often than once a day or for longer than 33 days. In fact, the more you listen to it, the more readily your basic self will integrate the new patterns you are establishing.

As an integral part of the guided meditation, you will need to come up with a "secret word." Think of it as a password, the key that

If you know that you are one with the source,

then you don't feel tense or needy.

You don't feel lack or pressure. You're poised.

You're silent. You're peaceful.

You can work harmoniously with anything that comes your

way and then let it go, because you are free.

opens the door to your basic self. Several times during the meditation, you will be asked to say your password silently. As you work with this practice, you will see how repeating this password assists you in establishing a more direct communication with your basic self, allowing for a more cooperative relationship.

Your password will actually consist of two words: a color and a physical object. You can choose any color of the spectrum. (Gold and silver, while not technically colors, also work well.) The object could be something from nature, such as a lake, a tree, an animal, or a bird. Or it could be an inanimate object, such as a diamond or a bell. The combination of color and object should be one that is unlikely to occur in everyday life. "Blue Lake," for example, would not fit the guideline, but "Purple Swan" or "Green Sky" would. Choose something that is pleasing to you.

As you repeat your password silently, touch the tips of your thumb to the tips of your first two fingers, forming an "O." After you have been doing this meditation for a while, all you will need to do is say your password and place your fingers in this position, and you will immediately feel an inner connection with your basic self. You may even find phrases from the guided meditation coming to mind. We recommend that you repeat your password silently throughout the day to reinforce the contact with your basic self and the new, positive habits you are developing.

Because the password is special to your basic self, we advise you not to reveal it to others. Your basic self is letting you into its

Inspiration comes from a level deeper than thought.
It comes when you are quiet:
when the mind is holding steady,
the emotions are calm,
and the body is in balance.
Then the Soul comes forward with its joyfulness.
When it does, the imagination comes with it.
As the mind lets loose, you may doubt yourself
and wonder if you're deluding yourself.

It's important to train yourself to recognize
the difference between your wishful thinking
and the inspiration that comes from
your divine nature and intuitive knowing.
To do this takes practice and learning to trust yourself.

domain with this key. If you treat the password casually, it will eventually lose its effectiveness, which may undermine the trust between you and this precious level of consciousness. Be sure to listen to the guided meditation where others cannot hear it, or use earphones.

There are different ways to work with the guided meditation. One is to find a quiet place where you can be relaxed but aware while listening to the CD. (If you tend to fall asleep when you lie down, find a comfortable sitting position.) This way, the conscious self and the basic self will both hear the meditation.

Another way to meditate with the CD is to listen with the sound turned down until it is barely audible. Then you can safely use the guided meditation as you go about your daily activities. (Exception: DO NOT listen to the CD while driving a car or operating machinery.) With the sound turned down, the conscious self may not hear the words, but the basic self will be aware of all the information. Similarly, if you fall asleep at night listening to the CD, the basic self will still hear the meditation.

You may find yourself moving in
and out of Soul consciousness many times.
The trick is to recognize when that shift happens
and still maintain Soul consciousness.
Until you can do that, it is okay to keep moving
in and out of Soul consciousness.
That will give you practice.
Practicing joy and loving is more fun
than practicing depression, anxiety, and fear.
Put yourself in training for Soul consciousness
by practicing the positive aspects of living and loving.

4

THE ROAD MAP

By now you may be thinking that "All this sounds great, but how do I do it? How do I live from Soul?" There are spiritual laws to assist us. If the very idea of laws bothers you, you'll be relieved to know that as you work with these spiritual laws, you'll discover that they give you a higher perspective, and so they actually help you relax and enjoy life more. In that sense, spiritual laws function like traffic regulations. Without traffic laws, driving would be a free-for-all of traffic jams and dangerous accidents. Just as traffic regulations help keep the cars and trucks moving safely and smoothly, spiritual laws provide guidance to keep our lives flowing smoothly and in the right direction.

Discovering the Soul is a continual process of leaving behind old, familiar patterns and venturing into the new. This can be difficult at times. When we are fearful or resistant, we contract, shutting the door to the true self. But if we can adjust our attitude and treat the journey to the Soul as an adventure, we will be rewarded with personal growth and more enjoyment. The key is a childlike outlook.

Never forget that you are more than what you do.
You are more than anything you teach.
You are more than anything you say.
You are more than anything you could ever express.
Always keep in mind that the
highest good will prevail
and that your main job
is simply to cooperate with it.
It's ironic, but the key to
being truly in control
is cooperation.

Child*like* is not child*ish*. A childish view is spoiled, immature, and personality-driven. Childlike, on the other hand, relates to qualities we associate with the heart: being open and honest, living in the present moment, trusting our intuition. As adults we can learn a lot from this approach. The child is not concerned with protecting his image and can, therefore, be a true learner, open and receptive to whatever comes his way. If we drop our concern with appearances and take each moment as it comes, instead of rehashing the past and worrying about the future, we, too, can greet life in the same innocent and trusting way. This approach can be challenging for people in a society like ours, which overemphasizes the intellect. Intellectuals often have difficulty letting go of their ideas about how life should be. Their minds constantly take them out of the moment and into efforts to analyze and manipulate the world around them.

When we are in harmony with spiritual laws, we can let go of our opinions and approach life with what Zen master Shunryu Suzuki called "beginner's mind": "In the beginner's mind there are many possibilities," he said, "but in the expert's there are few." We can live in the state of true play. What we generally call "play" are games of strategy. This form of play, whether in relationships or on the football field, is all about competition and one-upping others. But the true self's only game is the game of loving, which involves cooperation and caring. When we look at life from a true-self perspective, we continually discover new things about ourselves and others.

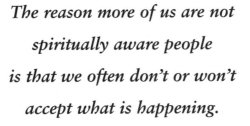

The reason more of us are not
spiritually aware people
is that we often don't or won't
accept what is happening.

While in our false-self state of awareness, we tend to focus on material things. We fantasize that if we had the right job, a great relationship, and enough money, life would be perfect. Ironically, the fulfillment of that "perfect-life" fantasy in reality has nothing to do with the outer world. Fulfillment is found in the contentment and joy we experience when we are living in the true self, irrespective of external conditions.

The Road Map referred to in the title of this chapter provides guidance in navigating the path to the Soul. The spiritual laws are the foundation of the map. Each law is a kind of marker along the way. When you can apply even one of these laws, you are on the right track to living from the true self.

THE FOUR SPIRITUAL LAWS

The four basic spiritual laws are Acceptance, Cooperation, Understanding, and Enthusiasm. Each can be applied in any situation to bring you back to your center and into alignment with your true self.

Acceptance

The first law of Spirit is Acceptance. This is one of the most important principles in the unfolding of spiritual awareness. Acceptance asks you to accept any situation as it is and to accept yourself as you are. You accept what is. The law of acceptance is actually very logical: when you set aside your feelings and thoughts and negative fantasies, *what is* is all that's going on.

You cannot control circumstances from the outside.

So instead of resisting pain and failure

and defending against it,

you can embrace and encompass

your pain and your failures,

fully accepting them

so that they become part of you.

You then can let them go

because they are part of your inner environment—

they are within your domain—

and the loving of your Soul can dissolve them.

Inner growth often comes through making mistakes, but many people can't make a mistake without self-castigation. The first spiritual law offers another choice: instead of condemning yourself for your missteps, you can accept them. We can seldom control what happens in life, but it is always within our power to choose our response.

When you're fretting about a problem, it usually means you're not accepting the situation. Similarly, when you're upset with yourself, it generally means you aren't self-accepting. When you are berating or judging yourself, you have strayed off the path to Soul. This is the moment to reach for the road map.

Acceptance doesn't mean that we agree with, like, or condone what is going on. The law of acceptance allows us to look at every situation as a stepping stone on the path to Soul and every situation as our teacher. Henry David Thoreau summed up this principle nicely when he wrote, "I came into this world, not chiefly to make this a good place to live in, but to live in it, be it good or bad."

In "Song of Myself" from *Leaves of Grass*, Walt Whitman offers another eloquent statement of acceptance:

> *I exist as I am, that is enough,*
> *If no other in the world be aware I sit content,*
> *And if each and all be aware I sit content.*
> *One world is aware and by far the largest to me*
>   *and that is myself,*
> *And whether I come to my own today or in ten*

When we surrender our
petty control patterns to our Soul—
which is on a higher and more refined level
than our minds, emotions, and bodies—
we transfer our consciousness
to what is really running things.
We then don't have to
make things happen in our lives.
They simply happen,
and our task is to cooperate
with the natural movement
inherent in all things.

thousand or ten million years,
I can cheerfully take it now, or with equal
cheerfulness I can wait.

Cooperation

Once you accept a situation, the next step is **Cooperation**. This is the second law of Spirit and another marker on the journey. Unconditional cooperation with whatever is happening is one of the keys to creating happiness and well-being. It is a powerful antidote to stress.

Cooperation has a lot to do with letting go. When we cooperate, not only do we let go of the need to be better than others, which reinforces the false self and ego, but we also let go of our resistance to change and to not getting our way. Once we have accepted the reality of *what is*, we can go with the flow. We stop trying to control other people or bend situations to our will. To get the idea of what this means, picture a surfer riding a wave. He's not trying to push the breakers or hold back the tides but to become so attuned to the movement of the water that he and the wave are one.

We don't like to admit when we're not being cooperative. If asked, most of us would say, "Of course I am. I get up every morning and go to work. I'm there on time. I keep my mouth shut and stay out of trouble. I'm cooperating." True, that's cooperation of a sort. But it's minimal, and it will probably get you minimal results. You may moan that life is unfair, that you don't deserve the bad things that happen to you. You may even be tempted to blame God for

You commit yourself to yourself—
not to the personality or the mind
or the emotions or the body or the wallet,
but to that very essence of God
that we identify as the Soul.

your troubles. But God didn't have anything to do with them. When you cry out, "Why me, God?" His reply might well be, "Because you put it in motion, and I love you so much that I allow you to experience and learn from it."

Perhaps you would like to have a more creative job, more money, closer relationships, or greater happiness. How might you be blocking the kind of cooperation that would bring those to you? Attitude is one big factor. When you are in a state of cooperation, your attitude is one of joy and enthusiasm. If you are asked to do something, you do it—and then some. You not only do the job at hand fully and completely, but you also look ahead to the next project. Your focus extends beyond yourself and your immediate needs and desires.

When your attitude is cooperative, you are always thinking, "What can I do for you that will assist you even more?" Your creativity comes to the fore. If, for example, someone asks you to close the door because they're chilly, you will not only close the door but also check the windows for drafts, turn up the heat, and offer them a sweater or anything else you can think of to make sure the person is comfortable. The proverbial "willingness to go the extra mile" describes the attitude of cooperation.

Understanding

The third law of Spirit is Understanding. After we accept what is and cooperate with it, understanding appears. Here, understanding is not a mental or intellectual process. Rather, it

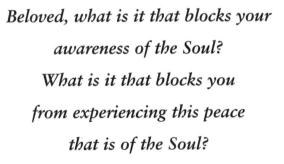

Beloved, what is it that blocks your
awareness of the Soul?
What is it that blocks you
from experiencing this peace
that is of the Soul?

means being centered, resting in the unconditioned true self, where there is no measure of "greater than" or "less than" anyone or anything else. This type of understanding brings peace and tranquility.

It is often said that it takes great courage to see the face of God. What is needed is the courage to see past what we think *should be* and move on to *what is*. This means seeing the world without negative judgment, even when the false self is saying, "I know a better way." It means seeing past our conditioning, which distorts reality to conform to the positions we take. The true source of our inner and outer conflicts is our failure to understand that we are the Soul. When we realize that God is present in everything, everywhere, and that the Soul is eternally present, the sense of conflict disappears.

When you move out of the present moment—the natural dwelling place of the true self—life can seem overwhelming. The best way to confront any new challenge is to slowly and lovingly expand your energy field to meet, then encompass, the situation. If you take challenges one at a time, extending your energy in this way will be easy. If at any time you feel overwhelmed, take a few moments to become still; then move into being patient. You may have to be patient for a day, a month, a year, simply observing the situation. But everything changes, and if you maintain a state of loving observation, you will be able to outlast the difficulty.

You can deal with any challenge in this way: lovingly extend your energy field and encompass the situation, then maintain a sense of

If you will strive to have a pleasant disposition
while you're doing whatever you're doing in the world,
there is a greater tendency for your Soul,
which is so perfect and so loving,
to radiate out of your pleasant disposition.
A truly pleasant disposition is loving,
compassionate, and empathic,
with the ability to know
what's going on in the world,
because it is not run by the ego.
If you take that same pleasantness
back inside you,
you live with an abundance of
enthusiasm that overflows to others.
Now, that is truly helping the planet.

neutral observation. This approach places you securely in your center, the Soul. Then, from this center, spiritual energy starts radiating outward. It does not radiate out as personality, but as an expression of your Soul's light.

Enthusiasm

The fourth spiritual law and the last marker on the road map is Enthusiasm. A first cousin of positive expectations, enthusiasm comes from the Greek word *entheos*, "having the god within." When we go deep inside—past our thoughts, emotions, and doubts—we can tap in to this spiritual energy and utilize it to improve our lives. We can also share it with others, making a tangible contribution to improving the world around us.

Riding our enthusiasm, we can accomplish things we never thought possible. Enthusiasm gives us the ability to stay focused and achieve what needs to be done with surprising ease. This is essential in today's frenzied world, where so often we rely on caffeine or adrenaline for an energy boost. Sure, we'll get a burst of energy from drinking a double espresso, or pushing ourselves to meet a deadline, but soon enough the effect wears off, leaving us exhausted. True enthusiasm is the natural way to energy that's long-lasting.

Does this enthusiasm ever wane? Yes, though it doesn't have to. True enthusiasm comes from participating with God's energy. When you're attuned to Spirit, this energy is unwavering. But unless you continually reconnect with the source, the spiritual

The mind cannot fathom the process for Soul.
You don't have to try to understand
something that is already within you.
You just have to awaken to your experience of it.
Then understanding appears.
The one who sleeps goes for abundance,
by manifesting illusion out of greed and insecurity.
The one who is awakened only has to
take their next breath and
discover the abundance
that is already present.

energy within you will dissipate and eventually disappear. Therefore, it's essential to take time for yourself. Time alone, in silence, allows your true self to reawaken and reconnect with the Divine. Then Spirit can flow through your body, mind, and emotions, generating enthusiasm on which you can ride.

In time, you'll learn to reconnect with this energy as quickly as you take your next breath. Breathing in awareness and breathing out enthusiasm becomes as regular as your heartbeat. As you make a habit of continually reconnecting to God's energy, the Soul replaces the personality as the center of consciousness. The Soul will still use the body, mind, and emotions as the vehicles through which it functions in the world. But instead of being distracted by your personality, you will be living in the crystal clarity of the Soul.

USING THE ROAD MAP

With the four spiritual laws as your guide, you can take any issue, situation, or challenge—relationships, health, finances, career, and so on—and move from a false-self view of it to the true-self perspective. (This process is particularly effective if you write down your answers. We also recommend you read appendixes 1 and 2 before starting this process.) Let's apply this method to a particular issue or situation that you are facing:

> State your false-self view of the matter. Include all the ways in which you are judging, blaming, and seeing yourself as a victim in the situation.

> Make a statement of acceptance about what is going on for you in this area of your life. Examples: It's all good.

When you are not aware of the Soul,
it is because you are blocking yourself.
Hard as it may be to believe,
no one else is blocking you.
If you sit back and just observe
whatever you perceive is blocking you,
you'll realize that it is your creation.
As you continue to observe it, and
to own your creation with loving neutrality,
you will move back into your Soul.

All is well. Be wary of the tendency to think conditionally, to say you'll accept this situation as long as something else takes place.

Make a statement of cooperation with the situation. Remember that true cooperation means going that extra mile. Example: I am going to flow with what is present and see what I can learn from the situation.

Make a statement of understanding about the situation. Example: Sometimes life is about being patient. I may not understand intellectually what is going on, but in my heart I understand that I am loved and that my Soul is present.

Make a statement of enthusiasm about the situation. Example: Everything that has been put in my life is for my good. I'm going to let go and enjoy it and to share my loving in complete freedom.

Bring your attention to the rising and falling of your breath. You may chant Hu as a way to attune yourself even more deeply to Spirit.

Ask for Light, for the highest good, to come into your Soul, to push out any upset, disturbance, imbalance, or disease, and then to surround you and fill you.

Sit in silence for one minute. Dwell quietly in your Soul, in your true self. Remember that the main qualities of the Soul are loving, peace, and joy. Without losing touch with your center, your true self, come back to the world.

We are so caught up in attachment to results
and our insecurity about what is happening
that we are blocking ourselves.
I wish I could get you to see
that you are the one blocking yourself.
Despite what it may look like,
no one else is blocking you.

If you would just be with whatever
seems to be blocking you,
you would realize that it is just an illusion
and really doesn't exist.
Observe the block until it comes
into harmony inside you.

Release and disperse what is no longer part of you.
What's left? The Soul, you.

Write down your true-self point of view about your situation. Note if your feelings have changed from when you were looking at the situation through the eyes of the false self.

It is very important to take full responsibility for what comes out of the true self as you write it down. If, while writing, you become anxious or judgmental or if you start to second-guess yourself, it is a sign that you have moved back into the false self and your ego-personality is again in the driver's seat. Repeat the exercise, this time going deeper with your issue or challenge. Remember that everything can be used for learning and personal growth and to uplift yourself and others.

Before you act on anything from your true self, it is of prime importance that you check it out. The true self will not direct you to do anything that would in any way hurt yourself or another. The true self's nature is loving, so check the information you hear, perceive, or intuit from your true self against the guideline that what you act on must be supportive and loving towards yourself and others.

As you dwell in the true self, consider the possibility that you are already the patient, loving, joyous person you have been looking for.

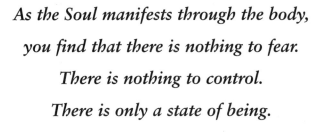

As the Soul manifests through the body,

you find that there is nothing to fear.

There is nothing to control.

There is only a state of being.

Practice
THE ROLE OF A LIFETIME

Now that you have the lay of the land beyond the territory of the false self with its Oscar-winning performances, take a moment to consider the following questions:

What would a new true-self script be like?

What would it feel like to have a new, clear, loving director?

As you explore these new possibilities, call to mind the qualities you've identified for your true self (see chapter 1), such as loving, peacefulness, joyfulness, and also use the four spiritual laws as your guide.

As you begin to rehearse your new role, you are likely to feel something like a gravitational pull back into the old one. Remember: it took decades to perfect the old performance, so give yourself time to practice your new lines. If you experience feelings of disorientation, take that as a good sign. It means that you are doing things differently and you are expanding and growing. Welcome the discomfort as growing pains. You're a butterfly breaking out of a cocoon.

Often friends and acquaintances may try to pull you back into your old role, even if unconsciously. You may have to lose these friends, at least temporarily, and find others who are more sympathetic to your efforts to master a new role. Your work or

Do your thoughts support the
direction or intention of your life?
Do they support moving into completeness,
into joy, humor, and fulfillment?
Rather than saying, "I need that chocolate cake,
I need that car, I need that dress, I need that house,"
move into the true essence inside you,
the truly aligned direction of your life.
Then all those other material things can appear
as a by-product, not as a focus.

One of the first steps into that true essence is to be silent.
In silence, intuition kicks in,
and we find that God is our source.
This is not the God of a little ego-personality approach,
but the real God, the very thing that you are.

home environment may also continue to support the old role. But if, in the midst of all these pulls and distractions, you can persevere in your new role, you will begin to observe changes in the world around you. What is changing, for the most part, are your perceptions. As we shift inside, external situations tend to shift as well.

There is a God part within each person.
That's the Soul. It is magnificent.
It is divine. It is not crippled.
It is perfect. It is aware.
And the Soul's nature is joyful.
When you experience joy,
you are experiencing your true self.

5

YOU, THE SOUL

Our goal is to move from the external power of the personality into the authentic power of the Soul. The personality expresses itself in how we use the exterior senses—not only in the way we hear, see, smell, touch, and taste but also in how and when we date, eat, shop, appreciate the arts, chat with friends, and persuade others to do what we want.

Because these exterior senses are guided by the personality, if your personality is at all distorted, the way you use your exterior senses will also be distorted. The personality becomes distorted primarily through our habits and addictions.

Most of our difficulties start with wanting things. The ego-personality—the false self—instinctively wants to smell and taste and touch and feel and hear and see. That wanting draws us into the world and worldly pursuits and sets us up to be disappointed, to feel the pain of being unfulfilled. This is part of the human condition. It's also the way we learn. If we don't get the lesson the

If you find yourself being blocked
in your pursuit of a particular goal,
you might be wise to step back,
take another look at your actions and motivations,
and reevaluate whether the goal is
for your highest good and
the highest good of those around you.

first time, we'll be given another opportunity—and another and another. If we still haven't learned, we might get counseling or educate ourselves through reading uplifting material, meditate, or go on retreat in order to put our senses back under our direction, rather than allowing them to direct us.

Every time our senses are drawn to something outside ourselves, our energy moves in two different directions. We can go ahead and do what our personality and senses want us to do, with no thought to the consequences. Or we can take the higher road and make a conscious choice to assume a more loving and caring approach to life.

In the previous chapter, we suggested that whenever you are confronted with a difficult choice, it's wise to ask yourself two simple but important questions:

If I choose to do this, what will be the effect of this choice on me?

If I choose to do this, what will be the effect of this choice on others?

Your answers will guide you toward making responsible choices. Responsible choices have loving and caring in them; personality choices often don't. Personality-based choices arise from our desires—from the wants of the ego, the false self. When we make a responsible choice, we bypass the personality and the senses and tap in to Soul energy. When we tap in to Soul energy, anger and greed disappear. Anger is the false self saying, "You're not doing what I want you to do." When someone doesn't do what we want, we often judge them and make them wrong. Judgments, as we've seen, come out of the false self.

If all our experiences were neutral,

what would that mean?

That our lives were sterile, a void?

No. "Neutral" is the loving heart, which is the Soul.

When the loving heart is flowing and functioning,

it has no wants and desires—none.

It is the emotions that want this and that.

When you're neutral and unattached,

you don't care what anyone else does.

But you care that you're loving and open

and that you're expanding your consciousness.

What if it doesn't expand at the rate you want?

You're not neutral as soon as you entertain that thought.

You're intellectualizing and

may be setting a trap for yourself.

Instead of listening to the intellect,

listen to your heart.

When we judge, our body lets us know that's what we're doing. We feel energy draining from the power center in the abdomen. In an effort to get our energy back, we experience fear. Fear is a call to action that triggers the release of adrenaline. When adrenaline kicks in, we feel a surge of power, but it is not authentic power. Authentic power comes from the Soul.

Unless there is real danger at hand, this call to action is the ego asserting itself. Whenever you react from the false self, you are setting yourself up for defeat. Inevitably, you will exhaust yourself and then attempt to regain energy by filling yourself with the nearest stimulant—alcohol, cigarettes, drugs, junk food. The false self perpetuates itself by saying, "What else could I have done?" The answer is that you could have made a choice from the true self instead.

But, you might ask, how does the false self, which doesn't even realize it has choices, make a true-self choice? The key is a positive shift in attitude. This is not "positive thinking," which can be negated by a negative thought, but *positive direction*, truly understanding that you are a spiritual being, a divine being who is living in the world. As a divine being, a Soul, you bring spiritual light and love into this world. You create a space for grace to be in your life. Grace is clear Spirit energy that comes to you without any conditions on it.

When you act out of the false self, there are all sorts of things you feel you must do, and they all take energy from you. When you

You practice being in the presence of Soul
by being flexible and open in your mind and emotions,
by looking at people
and loving the good and the bad equally.
Should you love others more than you love yourself?
No, because it is through loving yourself unconditionally
that you enter into the Spirit that resides within you.
That's when you become a real joy to be around.
That's when you discover the Soul.

live out of the true self, you draw on a source of infinite energy. But as soon as you give attention to your true self, your false self is likely to say, "Hey, what about me," and do anything it can to drag you back into the exterior senses. The true self doesn't say, "What about me?" The true self knows we must eventually return to it, so it is patient. It can wait, because it is eternal. The false self may be patient for a while, but it can't wait for long before it has to do something, then something else, and then something else. Living out of the false self, we become fragmented and procrastinate, not finishing what we started. Then we feel frazzled because life isn't going the way we think it should. When we finally look at the mess we've created, we once again rush to judge. But as we've seen, judgment is a serious matter. In judging our experience, we separate ourselves from our own divinity.

Yet the Soul is always standing by, waiting to be called, waiting for us to put our judgments aside. We can call upon the Soul right now. In this moment, we can forgive ourselves for forgetting we are divine. We can say, "God, Thy will be done." We can surrender the self-preserving nature of the false self and enter into the eternal life of the Soul—not as a religious concept, belief, or a hope, but as a living reality that exists in all of us.

Self-preservation is the false self speaking, expressing itself through ego concerns (What will happen to me?), relationship concerns (Who will love me?), money concerns (How will I get along in this world?), or a fear of poverty (What will happen if they take this from me?). In the world of the false self, we have to

The sun keeps rising and setting,

the moon keeps waxing and waning,

and in spite of all the messes

you get yourself into and all the trouble

you bring on yourself,

everything turns out okay.

Now, who do you think is doing all that?

be concerned with the effects of all our actions: "If I do this, then this will happen. Then if I do that, that will happen..." and so on, endlessly.

In the world of the true self, there's no need for such calculations. All we have to do is call on divine nature authentically—honestly, directly, forthrightly—by going within. The kingdom of heaven is within. The Soul resides within. Whether we call it prayer, meditation, silence, stillness, communion, or spiritual exercises, making contact with divine energy is the way to tap in to authentic power.

When we tap in to authentic power, we do not then need to become anything in the world. We just become present with the true self. The true self is joyful and loving. It needs nothing external to be joyful *about*.

The loving that is the true self's nature comes with sharing and caring. No matter how loving you feel, if you do not share your love, then you will simply be feeding your ego. But if you are caring and sharing, your loving opens the personality. Then the exterior senses can be utilized by the Soul, so that we naturally see where best to invest our efforts for the greater good of all.

The way of the Soul, of the true self, is not about doing things in order to get a return of some kind. When that is the basis of your actions, you may get the temporary satisfaction of a job well done, a new car, or a beautiful house. But you can have all the material

You do not have to seek love.

You are already love.

In Soul, you do not seek outside yourself

because who you are encompasses all there is.

True spirituality transcends all separation.

There is no lover because

there is no "other" to be loved.

There is only One.

That oneness is the Beloved.

wealth in the world, and if your motivation is not pure, you will feel hollow inside.

With your mind and imagination, you can see what the results will be if you act on your addictive impulses. In exercising your divine energy by making conscious choices, you allow Spirit to seal the door to your addictions, so that when harmful impulses tempt you, you won't act on them. You step free.

Here's how that works. As soon as the mean, ugly thing you don't want to see in yourself shows up, instead of contracting (closing down), you can remain open and, with compassion for yourself, say, "I am really sorry that I did that to myself. Now I want to do things differently, because I want different results."

Your behavior may not change right away. But whenever the addictive pattern rises up again, you can challenge it by not acting on it. You can ask the questions mentioned on page 107 and make a new, conscious choice toward a more loving and caring approach. Every time you challenge the addictive pattern, you strengthen yourself and empower the divinity of the Soul to become present in you as a natural source of energy, like breathing.

If, however, you give in to your addiction, it helps to remember that you're actually trying, in a roundabout way, to get love. Stopping at the bar, the chocolate shop, or the clothing store is a misguided way of saying, "I love me, and I feel love for me."

You don't necessarily feel blissful
when you are in the Soul.
You are very centered and
consciously aware of what is,
but you aren't experiencing an emotion per se.
You don't necessarily think of
what's happening when you're in the Soul;
you are clearly perceiving what is happening,
but it isn't a thought.
There aren't influences of the unconscious
or subconscious playing upon you
when you are centered in the Soul.
You are simply functioning from
a place of knowing direction.
It can be a very calm,
matter-of-fact,
solid place to be.

People kill themselves with their addictions, never realizing that what they are seeking is the awareness that Soul, not the body or personality, is who they really are.

We all have our battles, whether they are in the realm of the physical (health, careers, relationships, or finances) or the nonphysical (thoughts, imagination, emotions, or unconscious). Often we feel as if these challenges exist to belittle us, terrorize us, or even crush us. But they are only happening to the false self—the ego-personality—in the realm of the exterior senses. And all that is going to die someday. You might just as well let it die now and resurrect the Soul within you.

In the practice section of Chapter 2 *(Observe: It's All Equal)*, we suggested forgiveness as one of the pathways to the Soul. Forgiveness is not about you forgiving someone or even about you forgiving yourself for judging someone. If you do that, you're doing yourself a wonderful favor because that person will no longer be draining your energy. But there's an even greater forgiveness: It's about forgiving yourself for selling out to the exterior senses, i.e., not being loyal to your Soul and not having a wonderful, joyful interior life.

When you take all the energy that has been going out into the world and bring it back inside you, you get an intuitive glimpse of the whole concept of the Soul and the grace of God. Do you feel God loving you? If you do, you have pulled some of your exterior senses back inside you, and you're starting to build an awareness of Soul.

The only thing you can take with you is the loving,

detached state of Soul that gives you all things.

It sounds like a paradox, but one day many of you are

going to get up enough nerve not to possess things and to

find out how delightfully happy you are,

walking hand in hand with God, having all things.

Somebody will ask, "If it's yours, why don't you take it?"

You'll answer, "I don't have to take it because

it's mine already. I don't have to do anything with it.

You can use it, everybody can use it,

because in the last analysis, it's made of Spirit,

and that's where I'm living. It's not only mine; I'm it.

It's me." It becomes very, very simple.

The more awareness of the true self you can build, the more authentic power you will gain to sustain you in difficult times. If you can contain this energy and stop it from dissipating, you will begin to have a wonderful relationship with yourself. You will no longer be searching "out there" in the world for authentic power. You will know that it's inside of you. You can now live from the inside out. You will feel fulfilled, complete.

There are people who have a great deal materially but not much awareness of who they are. There are others who do not have much materially but have a great awareness of Soul energy; these people are wealthy beyond imagining.

We've so often heard: seek first the kingdom of heaven and that the kingdom of heaven is within. This is your place of healing. When you stop relying on the intellect and come to the wisdom of the heart, you access the door to divinity. The heart is the source of compassion and forgiveness.

When the body falls away, the Soul no longer has any personality-ego concerns pulling at it. But you don't have to wait until death to experience inner freedom. You can celebrate your freedom now.

God's power is inherent

in your being through the Soul.

It is the pearl of such great price that to reach it,

you must undergo a complete transformation

of consciousness and learn to take full responsibility

for what you put in motion.

You learn to complete what you begin.

If your creation is of the physical world, complete it here.

If it is of the imagination, finish it there.

If it's emotional, resolve it in the emotions.

If it is of the mind, finish your thoughts.

Don't start things you don't intend to finish.

Watch carefully your commitments in the world.

Keep them realistic,

and only make commitments you can keep.

When you do, you experience freedom.

Practice
APPLYING THE LAW OF ASSUMPTION

We make a lot of assumptions in life, and we can get into a mess by not checking them out and communicating clearly. We assume; things that we later find out aren't so.

But before we dismiss assumption altogether, we should look at its positive side, its spiritual counterpart. When your consciousness is crystal clear, you can assume things and *know* that they are so. This is an entirely different process from ordinary assumption. In the spiritual realm, first you know something, *then* you assume; you claim your knowing.

As you assume this knowing, you become Soul, you become love, you become joy, you become health. In your heart, you become all those things. Can you really become all those things? Do it now. Use the Law of Assumption for your upliftment and spiritual growth. Assume that you are healthy, assume that you are awake, assume that you are divine, assume that you have abundance. God didn't put us on Earth and say, "Beg." He said, "All I've got is yours."

When you live by the Law of Assumption, you cannot second-guess or doubt yourself. There must be crystal clarity inside you, a deep, certain knowing, not merely belief.

When you go to see the Soul,

you mostly see your thoughts and nothing else.

So you say, "There's nothing else.

If there were, I would be able to see it."

You can't see the Soul's existence

because it is wrapped up in you.

Your Soul is what keeps you alive, not your mind.

The mind, as strong as it seems,

is not always to be trusted.

The Soul is solid ground.

On the level of Soul, you don't grab.

You can't possess, and you can't hold on to anything.

Whatever you try to possess, you lose.

You can't even possess your own body.

But if you love yourself, if you love the Soul within,

you have access to all things.

We humans are experts at making negative assumptions: I'm unworthy; I'm terrible; I'm a failure; I'll never get anywhere; God doesn't love me. You can be equally successful at holding to your true direction and overcoming whatever distracts you. Here is how this practice works: whenever you experience a distraction—let's say, feeling unworthy—go back to your center, find the clarity within, and say, "Right now, through invoking the Law of Assumption, I assume that this feeling of unworthiness is gone and will stay gone. I'm busy doing other things. I don't have time for this distraction."

The part of us that keeps the spiritual Law of Assumption from working is the ego. The false self uses the power of the mind and the emotions, backed by willpower and the power of the body, to prevent us from manifesting wonderful things in the world. But there's a bigger will, the Soul. Once you connect with the Soul, the ego seems like nothing. You wonder why you allowed your life to be run by such an inconsequential thing!

If you start assuming that you are Soul, you will become Soul, the Beloved. This is not something that will happen in some future time and place. It is true right here, right now.

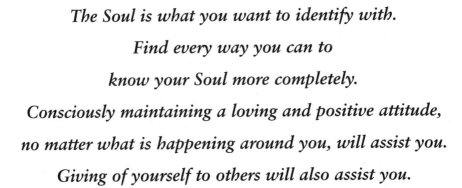

The Soul is what you want to identify with.
Find every way you can to
know your Soul more completely.
Consciously maintaining a loving and positive attitude,
no matter what is happening around you, will assist you.
Giving of yourself to others will also assist you.
There are lots of ways to attune
yourself to the Soul. Experiment.
Find the ways that work for you and
that give you a sense of oneness with
everything and everyone.

6

ARE YOU THE SPIRITUAL SKY?

As we go through our everyday lives, it often appears that the false self—the personality—is very large, while the true self is very small. In reality, it's just the reverse. Once we connect to our true self we find that the space inside of us is more vast than we could possibly imagine. That space can metaphorically be called "the spiritual sky." Let's explore how we can relate to that inner vastness.

Even when we realize at some level that the mind is not the path to the true self, the false self is conditioned to believe that if we *think* something, it must be true. (Knowing how frequently we change our minds should make us question that assumption, but then the next thought comes along, and the next...and there we go again.)

What are thoughts, anyway? When we say, "I have this thought," what does that really mean? If we watch clouds in the sky, we can get some idea of what thoughts are or, at least, how they behave. Clouds, like thoughts, never stay still. As they move across the sky,

If you see disturbance in the world,

it is a reflection of disturbance in you.

If you see something you don't like in another person,

it is because that same quality exists

in you and you recognize it.

All your experiences, all your relationships,

reflect you back to yourself,

so that you can learn to know yourself

and accept yourself in greater and greater ways.

they morph into different shapes. One moment, you might look at a cloud formation and see a horse; the next moment, a woman's face. Similarly, as thoughts arise in the mind, they assume different forms according to our conditioning and desires. And when you inquire very deeply into what thoughts are and where they come from, you can begin to see that it is not "thoughts" you are looking at but a thought and a thought and a thought, a series of thoughts, a sequence of events.

When we have a series of thoughts, we say, "There is a mind." But the mind is as elusive as thought. You know that you think, but can you find the mind? No, because it does not exist. So we take a nonexistent something—the mind—that we know thoughts pass through, and we conclude, "This concept came from my thoughts, which came from my mind." Now we've inferred the existence of a mind that is not there. And then we go on to say things like, "My mind's made up." But how can you make up your mind if there's no mind to make up?

By now, you're probably thoroughly confused. But what I'm doing is giving you an opportunity to look at your "thought-ing" process, how you put thoughts together. The more we take these aggregations called thoughts and meditate on just one thought— or even a single word—the easier it becomes to separate thoughts into *a thought here and one here and one here.* Then the question becomes, what is between the thoughts? We discover that in the gaps between thoughts is the energy the thoughts ride on. This means that what is holding the thoughts is stronger than the thoughts themselves. The revelation is astounding.

The intuitive knowledge of the Soul

and its divine nature is always present.

Everyone has that knowledge deep within them.

If Spirit cannot be perceived mentally, emotionally,

physically, or through the unconscious, what's left?

Intuition. You can be intuitively aware of Soul and Spirit.

You just know. Then, when you're in the Soul,

you are the Soul, so intuition is no longer necessary.

If there is something stronger than the thoughts, why do we make our thoughts so important? Why do we cling to them so tightly, saying, "This is *my* thought—all *mine.*" Why do we get so self-righteous and judgmental about something that doesn't have any substance in the first place?

As these cloudlike thoughts float through the sky of our being, we give them form and meaning. Then we use those thoughts to give us strength. Yet the true source of strength is not the thoughts but our spiritual being, the energy the thoughts ride on. It is in the space between thoughts that we find bliss, not in the thoughts themselves. If you are sitting here now, thinking how blissful you are, you aren't, in fact, blissful. You are *thinking* about bliss, not *being* blissful. The thought of bliss is not bliss. It is only another cloud floating in the sky.

Something similar happens when you say you want to quiet your mind. How can you do that if there is no mind? "Okay," you counter, "then I'll quiet my thoughts." But how can you quiet your thoughts when the thoughts aren't yours to begin with? And while you're wondering about that, another thought might occur to you: Who is it who's doing the wondering?

Finally, an answer: It's you—your true self, your essence, the spiritual sky—who wonders. As you gather your thoughts together and go over and over them, you become so closely identified with them that when you look at the world, that's what you see: your thoughts about the world. Then, as you live in this

Whatever has happened in the past,

with whomever, over whatever, is past.

It is as simple as that because it's past.

And whether they were right or wrong,

whether you did or you didn't do it,

whether they did or they didn't,

is absolutely immaterial.

Don't waste your time on it.

world you've constructed with your thoughts, you do all sorts of things to prove it's real. That's how you get trapped in the false self. Who you really are is that vast expanse that can exist in all sorts of states and conditions. Yet you often choose to hold on to a really restricted point of view, making that your reality while you deny that you are the whole sky.

When we talk about the sky, we say the earth has a sky. But isn't it possible that it's the other way around and that the sky has an earth? We are that great invisible expanse—the spiritual sky—and within us we have thoughts and feelings, just as the sky contains clouds and planets and stars. If you can move your awareness into the spiritual sky and see that you encompass the earth and the clouds and beyond and that you are at one with them, then you are close to experiencing your true self. If you can live in that spaciousness for even a few seconds, you will have direct experience of your divine nature.

So, are you ready now to live in the spiritual sky that is always present? Or do you contract into the false self with thoughts like "I'm not worthy;" "I'm nothing;" "I don't have enough money;" "I need a better relationship"? When you realize you are the spiritual sky, you can live in the presence of whatever thoughts and feelings you have, even if you can do no more than love and accept them.

Remember the thought of wanting a new car? You got the new car, and it was great. Then two years later you traded it in. What happened to the thought about how great the new car was?

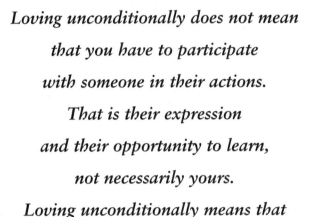

Loving unconditionally does not mean
that you have to participate
with someone in their actions.
That is their expression
and their opportunity to learn,
not necessarily yours.
Loving unconditionally means that
you accept their action without judgment
and without being emotionally reactive.

Another thought took its place. A new model came out, and you wanted that one, or your old car got a few dings. We've always got a perfect explanation for why we do things, but the truth is, we do what we want and then make up a story to justify it.

We become attached to our thoughts—and our explanations of and justifications for what we think—because we're not dwelling in a space where ideas can arise, float, then fade away. If you can find that sacred space within that is present here and now, you will be able to witness the you who observes the comings and goings of the world in a detached way. Detached doesn't mean uninvolved. In fact, when you live in the spiritual sky, you become so fully involved in life that people assume you are attached to it.

They may say things like, "I didn't think you would ever leave that job. I thought you would be there till you died." *I thought this. I thought that.* Who cares what they thought? In a moment they're going to think something else.

When thoughts come along, I just observe them, like clouds passing across the sky: *There's that. Then there's that. Then there's that.* Sometimes the clouds are black and rain-filled. Then I say, "That's a black rain cloud." Someone else might look up at the sky and say, "Wow, I'm glad it's raining today! The vegetables and fruit trees really need water." Still another person might say, "Oh, it's raining today. That's terrible. I'm so depressed."

Your health, your awareness, your freedom,
your spiritual liberation are all with you right now.
All of that resides within you.
You, however,
cannot hold your focus or your concentration
on that realization long enough to receive it,
because you have conditioned yourself
with mental fixations and emotional doubting
and tremendous expectations of
what you think other people should do
(which can be one of the most foolish fixations going).

Who is correct? Is one view better than the others? Or is what's happening just clouds (and minds) doing what clouds (and minds) do?

The more we can let go of our ideas about right and wrong, the less we will get caught up in righteous indignation, which is just a thought about what somebody is doing to us. We read someone's opinion on a piece of paper and then let those thoughts control the sky. We are only too willing to allow the tiny false self to eclipse the infinite true self, the spiritual sky. Our essential being can never be destroyed. As you live in the spiritual sky, you will observe your problems floating by and disappearing. And you will be living in the fullness of the true self.

There *is* one positive thing we can do with our thoughts: we can use them to keep remembering who we are—loving beings. It's so easy to get caught up in the stress of life today and forget that. We rarely stay focused on an idea for three seconds before our attention spins off into other thoughts, often negative ones of depression, anxiety, rejection, and fear. Then the body tenses up.

Wouldn't it be nice if our bodies were relaxed and peaceful, our emotions joyful, and mentally we were free? Freedom isn't the license to do what you want; it's the ability to be who and what you are—until you realize that you are the sky and that you are connected with and part of the very essence of all things. Then you don't have to play the game of separation, lack, or unworthiness. You open to the essence of who you are, which is much greater

The very one you're looking for is in your heart,
and the very one you've been after has always been here.
And if you really get that, it stirs deep inside you,
beyond any place of comprehension,
and goes to the place of understanding.
That is the place where you say,
"Yes, yes, yes, yes."

than any thought or feeling. And you awaken to the knowledge
that the spiritual sky is all of us.

If I judge any part of you,
I am honoring my judgment
more than I am honoring
the Soul inside you or me.
That would be shutting off my Soul,
and I won't do that to myself.
I suggest that you don't do that to yourself either.

Practice

THE SACRED SPACE WITHIN

The spiritual sky is the sacred space within you. Once you are in touch with it, you become very relaxed and peaceful, yet dynamically aware. The spiritual sky is a holiness you carry with you, and the more you inhabit it, the less inclined you will be to give up the space to judgments, fears, or negative habits.

As with most spiritual practices, it is important to begin this one by bringing your full attention to the present moment. Your breath can assist you in this. By simply observing your breathing, you can bring yourself to a receptive and relaxed state in a very short time. Here is an example of how to approach this practice:

- Focus on the rising and falling
  of your breath for 10 seconds.

- Let your awareness expand beyond
  your body to fill the space you are in.

- Experience yourself being held by that space.
  Lean forward a little and feel the support.
  Then lean back a little back and again feel
  the space hold you.

- Your mind and your emotions are being held
  by this space in a similar way. As you become

The Soul is your connection to God's loving heart.
The Soul is living water to quench your thirst.
The Soul is living food to nourish you.
The Soul is the living breath that gives you life.

attuned to your body, mind, and emotions
being held by this space, you will feel more
confident about letting go of bodily tension,
emotional worry, and mental preoccupations.

■ Now bring that sense of space inside you.
Sometimes it will seem like a bubble of
clear light. As you maintain awareness
of this sacred space, you will start to
feel relaxed and centered.

■ Throughout the day, see if you can hold
on to this sense of sacred space inside you.
It is easy to give the space away to a negative
thought, a distraction, a stressful event,
or getting someone's approval. When that
happens, simply bring yourself back to this
sacred space by reminding yourself that you
are the spiritual sky.

As you continue to work with this practice, you will begin to
observe how you give your center away. Perhaps you allow
yourself to be ruffled by a slow-moving line at the airport, a traffic
jam, a disagreement with your spouse or co-worker, or misplacing
your car keys when you're late for an appointment. Ask yourself,

*Is this really worth losing my peace of mind
and compromising my health and well-being?*

As you become more attuned to the sacred space within, you will
become less and less inclined to give it up to passing thoughts or

We shut down our awareness of God
by putting our faith in the world,
professing God's greatness out there.
But God's greatness isn't out there. It's inside us.

irrelevant distractions. Remaining calm and relaxed will no longer be a matter of discipline; it will be a pleasure. Being with your true self will be your highest priority.

When the personality looks at abundance,

it sees it as quantity.

The Soul views it differently:

it sees abundance as quality.

If you have a hundred lovers and

none of them genuinely loves you,

what is the value in all that quantity?

What looks like abundance is really emptiness.

But if you have one person who is fully present,

loving, and uplifting you, that's true abundance.

7

THE SEA OF GRATITUDE

Those of us living in the West today enjoy a standard of living more privileged than anywhere else in the world. But despite better health, more wealth, longer life, and our many other advantages, we don't seem to be any happier than our forebears. Despite all we have, our expectations are ever rising. What we face as a culture is a pervasive feeling of lack.

One of the approaches to life that ties us into the true self is gratitude. It's the spiritual antidote to a feeling of lack. But we may not allow ourselves to appreciate the abundance around us. Our increased expectations often lead to increased disappointment. We may endlessly complain: "I don't have enough;" "They have more than me;" "They're not doing enough for me;" "There won't be enough when we get there;" "The world is falling apart." Day in, day out, we tend to focus on what we lack.

The true self, however, has no concept of lack. It's the false self that wallows in thoughts of not having—or being—enough. We

To anchor yourself in the past as a point
of refuge or security is to drag anchor
in this whole process that is life.
You'll never really get out into the ocean
to see what is going on.
To project yourself into the future
means you will never have fulfillment in the present.
If God is delivering everything now
(and believe me, that is so),
why are you concerned with the past or future?

often behave as if those thoughts are real, when in fact, we always have something to be grateful for.

Swimming in the sea of gratitude is like swimming in the ocean. When you relax into it and let it support you, it becomes a weightless and buoyant affair. To get into this mind-set rapidly, try this experiment. Think of something you are profoundly grateful for. It could be something you own that you treasure; it could be a nurturing and supportive relationship, or children you love very much. It could involve being grateful for something that could have happened but didn't: an accident from which you emerged unharmed, a serious illness that you or a loved one recovered from. It's important that it be something deep and meaningful because you are going to tap in to that experience now. As you do that, experience the feeling of gratitude that comes over you. Notice the relief and release in your body, mind, and emotions that come with the feeling of gratitude. This is a dynamic tool for relieving stress. You are focusing on what is really important to you and leaving behind, at least for that moment, the often petty distractions of life. As you keep focused on the gratitude for what is most important to you, it will give you a higher perspective on life. A higher perspective is relaxing and expansive, and enables you to see your life situations more clearly.

It's a spiritual axiom that we attract what we dwell upon, so if we dwell upon lack, that's what we'll get. To lose the feeling of lack, we come back to the Soul, the true self, and dwell upon the abundance that is immediately present and all

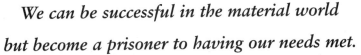

*We can be successful in the material world
but become a prisoner to having our needs met.
So we continually have to
manifest something to meet our needs
and, in the process, the inner life is ignored.
We may have lots of money,
but we lack true abundance.*

around us. This is the abundance that God is giving us right now. It may be as simple as the next breath we breathe or a piece of fruit we bite into and feel grateful to have.

Many people see abundance in terms of having what they want when they want it. But that's the false self's approach. When I refer to God's abundance, I'm talking about taking time to look around you with joy and gratitude, taking in this moment in its fullness, knowing that God is present right now, and appreciating the blessing of being alive.

When we swim in the sea of gratitude, we recognize that God's abundance is all around us. When we live in the true self, we see that whatever is manifesting in our lives is manifesting out of God's abundance. God never manifests lack.

When we manifest out of the false self, what we attract comes out of our desires. We may have the illusion that we've accomplished something because we've gotten what we wanted. But we may not have grown spiritually. When an opportunity for success comes our way, we're likely to fail, because we haven't prepared the inner ground to receive it. Success requires an open, fertile space to sprout—not the meager patch of arid soil that accompanies a feeling of lack.

If you look at your work situation and wonder, "Will I make money next year?" or "Will I have a job next year?" the answer is, "Probably not," because you're manifesting lack. You're

Why is it regarded as unusual
to own up to how good you are,
how spiritual you are,
how beautiful you are?
People will readily own up to
how bad they are, how stubborn
and full of guilt and anxiety they are,
how they screwed things up,
and how they're wasting their life.
So why not the positive?

creating it with every breath. Imagine, instead, saying to yourself, "Next year I'll have a job. I don't care if it's *this* job. But it will be a job that is abundantly alive and fun and that is awakening me to my true self. God will help me be strong enough to fulfill it in the greatest way possible. And right now, I'll learn and get strong so that when the job comes I'll be prepared." See the difference?

God's abundance doesn't come on your timetable. It comes on God's. So your task is to manifest patience. When you ask for anything, whether spiritual or material, you must be willing to give in order to receive. You must be willing to make the first overture, the first presentation, the first gesture of giving. Giving is how we grow spiritually. When we give from the heart, from the true self, we create the open space to receive more. This is not more in material terms. The "more" we receive is more gratitude, a greater ability to know our blessings.

We don't give out of our lack; we give out of our gratitude. We don't give in order to receive more (that's a sign of greed); we give from our fullness, our overflow. As divine beings, we are already full. When we live in gratitude for what we have, there is only this fullness. The false self thinks in terms of "full" and "not full," but the true self simply manifests fullness all the time.

That fullness gives of itself; it radiates from you. When you are living in the true self, in the fullness, you simply do what is in front of you, taking the next step and doing what needs to be done. That is what it means to live a spiritual life. As you do this, you will find

To have abundance in Soul

does not mean having lots of things;

it means having access to,

and communion with,

the essence of all things.

Once you are in touch with that,

you have all things inside you.

You don't feel any lack.

You have fullness and gratitude,

and you walk free,

knowing that whatever you need

will come to you.

that more abundance comes to you and, in turn, you are able to give even more.

Many people feel they must have the latest car or gadget. They go over and over in their minds the list of things they want. But living a life of gratitude is not about what you feel or think; it's about doing, about action. Most of us react instead of act. We are inclined to take rather than give. Instead of being grateful, we look for other people to bring us abundance. That approach, which comes out of the ego-personality, can greatly limit what comes to us.

When you subtly beg others to rescue you—"Please give me money. Please give me this or that"—you are looking for abundance to come from outside yourself. This disempowers you as a spiritual being, because you are essentially telling yourself that you, a Soul, are not enough. So you start to lose the authentic power that comes from within you. Most people look for outer material things to fulfill themselves inwardly, but it is by tapping in to the authentic power within that you grow spiritually, access your true self, and find lasting fulfillment. You have to know deep down that abundance is present inside of you. That starts with being grateful for what you have right now. Many very rich people I know don't feel that they have enough. The false self is never satisfied.

If you want to improve your attitude of gratitude and thereby manifest abundance, one important step you can take is to complete what you have started. Loose ends subtly drain your energy and distract you, giving you a sense of lack. Being complete

We manifest
not by trying to attract
the things of the world to us
but by giving.
When we share our essence,
good things come to us automatically.
We don't have to manipulate,
play games, con people, or lie to them.
We can just be our naturally loving self.

and up-to-date with what comprises your life—relationships, finances, health, and so on—forms a solid foundation that will give you a greater sense of security because you will be able to trust yourself. Self-trust begins with keeping your word to yourself and completing whatever is draining your energy. This prepares you to see yourself as a grateful, abundant being—not as an ideal but as a living reality.

As you tie up the loose ends in your life, something interesting happens, and you may very well find that the old ways don't work. This is your Soul calling you to move to a higher level of awareness and responsibility. If you don't want to let go of the old, negative ways because they seem to be getting you what you want, you are not living in true abundance. You are identified with material possessions, with what you have and own and think is yours. But what is truly yours is not here on Earth; it is in the Soul. When you realize that, you once again move into gratitude for whatever is present in your life. No longer motivated by your negative desires, you strive to manifest "for the highest good of all concerned."

We have to get out of our own way in order to allow God's abundance to manifest. When we manifest abundance from within, our true needs are met. We no longer seek abundance in external form, but we come to the very essence of what it is inside us—the true self—and realize we already have what we need. That's a wonderful moment, knowing that your supply is not in another person or in your environment, but is in God, the Beloved,

You are placed on the planet
with everything you need already inside you.
You can't be upset unless you allow it.
You can't be controlled unless you allow it.
This puts you in a unique position.
You are a creator.
You can create
discord or harmony,
despair or happiness,
depression or joy,
lack or productiveness.

who resides inside of you. And that source, that inner supply, is infinite. Once you know that, you can tap in to your own wellspring of joy at any time.

We're always drawn to people who demonstrate abundance. They're the ones whose shoulders we cry on. Abundant people know we all go through times of stress when we're growing, when we're breaking out of old patterns into the new, and they give us an abundance of understanding. They see past our mistakes and love us anyway. Their abundance gives; it doesn't take.

A person in lack will fulfill your lack. It's like the old saying "misery loves company." We come to a point, however, when we hit bottom and say, "Well, I don't have to fear failure. I've got an abundance of it. Now I'm carefree. I've got nothing to lose. I might as well go for everything." And that's the manifestation of abundance: to not be afraid of losing it all; to not be afraid of failing. You're free because you know that fulfillment is inside of you. Your wealth is your true self.

When we look at manifesting abundance, it is important that we don't fall into the downward spiral of never being satisfied. An attitude of gratitude is essential. I'd rather have a telephone that's hard to hear on than no telephone. I'd rather have fluoridated water than no water. You can learn to appreciate even your irritation and negativity. Then, no matter what happens, you're a grateful person. That grateful feeling has a wonderful, protective quality to it. Gratitude is a higher state of consciousness that keeps

There is no room in the Soul for unworthiness.

To be abundant on the Soul level
does not mean having access to many things,
but having access to the essence of all things
and being in communion with that one essence.

Manifestation results in a change of consciousness,
not necessarily in the ability
to make a physical form appear.

You have the essence of love inside you,
fully present and formless.
You do not need someone else to reflect love to you; you
can experience it directly from the Soul.

you free of opinions, thoughts, and feelings that do not have the quality of being grateful.

Even when life seems to be going badly, you can always find something to be grateful for: food on the table, a good friend, this breath. Some people like to recount at the end of the day the things in life they are grateful for. Others keep a gratitude list or journal as a reminder. Those are good methods, but there is an even better approach, which is to be grateful for *everything*. To live in a completely grateful way is to live a profoundly joyful life. It's as if you are swimming in a sea of gratitude, which supports and sustains you. One of the greatest miracles is being thankful for what you have right now. As Albert Einstein said: "There are only two ways to live your life. One is as though nothing is a miracle. The other is as though everything is a miracle"

When you focus completely on being grateful for your next breath, you'll find that most of your problems disappear in that instant. Keep that instant going: be grateful for whatever is around you right now. Every time you are in a state of gratitude, you radiate a positive energy that is contagious.

Once you've learned to manifest true abundance, you have the opportunity to share it with everyone as an expression of your gratitude. That means with yourself as well. The Bible said that we are all gods, we are all abundant, we are all creators. You can go out and create all sorts of jobs and all sorts of money, yet still remain closed. Sure, you manifested, but how many people did you run over in the process? True manifestation reveals your very

The mind stops at the limit of the mind;
the emotions stop at the limit of the emotions;
the imagination stops at the limit of the imagination.

This may seem obvious, but it is amazing how many
people think that they can use their emotions to solve
mental problems and use their minds to find God.

These elements of consciousness are just tools.
Tools need a guiding hand to do their work correctly.
And that guiding hand needs to be a loving one.

being, your Soul. You identify with the trueness of you, not with your personality, mind, emotions, or body, but with the divine center within, the "I am that I am." The true self is not affected by time or space, or change, or outside pressure. It knows neither lack nor desire. It is sufficient in itself. When we manifest correctly, we're manifesting ourselves. What else is there? The self is me, and it is you. It is God. All we have to do is manifest as a Soul, not a personality; not as someone trying to attract things, but as someone expressing goodness to others. One of the clearest signs of the Soul essence, the true self, is that it is giving.

Moving your inner awareness into your Soul is easy,

but it's just as easy to lose that awareness.

You can fall out of awareness

because the world doesn't seem to

support spiritual awakening.

Spirit lets you in easily,

but It has to give way

to the materiality of the world.

The material world has a billion distractions,

so it's necessary to watch where you place your focus

and your motivation for creating what you want.

If you want to know God, keep your eyes on God.

Practice

EXERCISING YOUR SOUL

After contemplating the quotations throughout this book and spending time with the other practices, you may be beginning to experience yourself as a spiritual being. The following practice is for going deeper, to the place where the Soul energy gathers inside you.

This place, located behind the center of the forehead, close to the pineal gland in the center of the head, is acknowledged as an important energy center by many mystical and spiritual traditions. Some call it the third eye; others, the Tisra Til; still others, the sixth chakra or the Holy of Holies.

The Holy of Holies was the most sacred room in the ancient Hebrew temple in Jerusalem. Only the high priest was allowed to enter. Churches, synagogues, mosques, and other places of worship are outer representations of the true place of worship: our own physical body, the temple of the Soul. To dwell in the sacredness of God, we don't have to go anywhere but within ourselves.

Before you start this practice, you will want to read appendixes 1 and 2 so you have the information you need to do the practice. After you've read the appendixes, find a quiet place to sit, and then place your attention at the third eye. Call in the Light of God to

We all fall and we always will,

as long as we have a physical body.

But so what?

How often you fall is not important;

what matters is how fast you can pick yourself up.

If you're wise, you won't struggle against what

is established on this physical level.

You'll work within it as you seek to

gain greater attunement with your Soul.

come into your Soul, to push out any negativity or imbalance, and to surround and fill you for the highest good.

Take a minute or two and silently chant Hu. Then, sitting in the silence of your heart, listen.

You may hear sounds. At first, you may hear a high-pitched tone similar to the sound you might hear near high-voltage electrical wires. This can be the response of your nerves relaxing and releasing. As you go deeper, you may hear the sound of Spirit—the Sound Current of God. This sometimes sounds like a babbling brook or the surf or violins or a flute. You may also experience inner movement, a feeling that you are floating upward or flying. Think of this as the Soul traveling through the dimensions of Spirit. You may see different colors, each one representing a different dimension.

On this inner journey, it helps to have a guide to show you the way. Fortunately, one is available in your own heart. This guide, which can be referred to as the Mystical Traveler Consciousness, has been known by many names throughout the ages. The Mystical Traveler Consciousness—The Traveler for short—is not something external. It is within each of us. The inner spiritual journey can be regarded as an ongoing awakening to the Mystical Traveler Consciousness on all levels, up to the heart of God.

There is no way to intellectually grasp the way the Traveler works. We cannot perceive the infinite with the finite mind. When

There is no path in spiritual progression.

There is just spiritual progression.

When people talk about a path,

they set up a distance

and a sense of beginning and ending.

That's a fallacy.

There is no beginning, no ending, and no separation.

You are never outside of God, whatever you do,

but if you express yourself negatively,

you may separate yourself from your awareness of God.

Express loving in all ways, always,

and you will know the presence of God in your life.

you come to know the Mystical Traveler Consciousness in your heart, that understanding comes from an intuitive place, not from the mind.

Move to the temple of the Soul within. Ask for the Traveler to be present with you for your highest good. As you focus inwardly, you may see a purple light at the center of, or to the right of your inner visual field. That light is often a sign of the Traveler's presence. Not seeing it does not mean it is not there. Just continue to ask for it, as you do this practice, and in time you will sense the Traveler's presence and see its light.

Now you have all you need for your journey to the true self, to your Soul. Blessings be with you, for they are present.

Baruch Bashan (the blessings already are).

APPENDIX 1

The HU Chant

A very effective means to focus the mind and open to your loving is chanting. Since the beginning of time, religious and spiritual groups have made a practice of intoning sacred words, sounds, prayers, and songs. Chanting builds up a powerful field of spiritual energy that can change your consciousness. The key is your intention: bringing an attitude of reverence and love to whatever you are chanting.

Sacred words are specific sounds or syllables that invoke a spiritual essence. As you chant, you can bring that essence, or vibration, into your own being. I recommend chanting Hu. Hu (pronounced like the man's name, Hugh) is a name found in Pali and Sanskrit, ancient sacred languages of southern Asia, that is used to refer to the Supreme God. Chanting Hu silently or aloud, alone or in a group, helps create attunement, bring you into spiritual alignment, and give you a sense of peace. As with other practices in this book, you don't have to hold any specific beliefs to do it. Try it, and see if it works for you.

Hu may be chanted in several ways. One way is to separate it into its letters "H" and "U," chanting a long "H" and then shifting to "U." If you are chanting out loud, take in a deep breath and, as you breathe out, chant "H" then "U." If you are chanting silently, you might intone the "H" as you breathe in, and the "U" as you breathe out. Another way to do this is to pronounce the "Hu" as one syllable (pronounced "Hugh") and chant it as you breathe out. Before you begin, sit quietly for a moment and allow your body to relax. Call in the Light to fill, surround, and protect you for the highest good (see Appendix 2 The Light).

Now begin the Hu sound. Take a deep breath, and as you exhale, chant HUUUUUUUUUU on one continuous note, until all the breath is expelled. Repeat 5 to 10 times, chanting HUUUUUUUUUU each time you exhale.

Then relax for a moment, watching and listening inwardly as you keep your attention on the rising and falling of your breath. You may also bring your attention to the middle of your forehead or to the top of your head.

Whenever your mind takes off in thought or your imagination soars in fantasy, you can use the Hu chant or focus on your breathing to bring yourself back to the present moment. As soon as you notice your mind wandering, gently direct your attention back to the object of your focus, the Hu sound or the breath. You may have to repeat this process often. It is natural for the mind to wander, so be patient with yourself.

If it seems as if nothing is happening, don't be concerned. The important part of all this is your intention to check it out by doing it to the best of your ability and observing your experience. Then observe. Give yourself enough time to work with it. Be patient. Be devoted to your own upliftment and unfoldment.

When you were a baby learning to walk, you didn't scold yourself when you fell down. You got up and tried again. Falling is just part of the process of learning to walk. This is the model for how we learn anything, including how to live. It's all about bringing ourselves back to the present, again and again. We love, then forget to be loving, then remember, and become loving again. The more we remember to love, the more habitual loving will become. It's a matter of being present in every moment.

APPENDIX 2

The Light

The Light is a spiritual force, an emanation of God that can be used as a practical tool for day-to-day living. When I refer to the Light, I mean the very highest and purest Light that exists. The Light is present everywhere and in everyone. It is always available to you. But in order to gain assistance from the Light, you have to ask for it. Since this Light is everywhere at all times, when you "ask" for it, what you are really doing is asking *yourself* to be present with the Light. You are bringing your awareness to the Light. In that respect, working with the Light is similar to practicing conscious breathing. You are always breathing, but *consciously* bringing your awareness to your breath can be transformational. So it is with the Light.

As you attune to the Light, if you say silently, "I ask for the Light for the highest good," this will bring in a form of support or protection for you. If there are situations or people you are concerned about, you can place them into the Light and then let go, confident that the Light is with them. As you release problems into the Light, you may actually feel them lift from you, leaving you freer inside.

Asking for the Light is a very effective and practical tool for letting go of your worries and concerns. It is a way of becoming present with the spiritual force of God. Here is a Light prayer that you can say at the beginning of the day, or whenever you feel you need more clarity or assistance in your life. Start by sitting quietly and spending a few seconds relaxing with your breathing. Allow your mind and body to come to rest. Silently repeat the following words, or your own variation on them:

> Dear God, I ask just now for the Light of God, the highest, purest Light, to be with me now, to surround me, to fill me, to fill this room or this space for the highest good. I ask that the Light go ahead of me this day so that I may grow inside and let go of anything that is no longer working for me. I ask that my heart be opened to loving. I ask that the Light be sent to my loved ones for the highest good.

If there are individuals you wish to place into the Light, you can silently say their names. If you are struggling with a particular problem, you can place that situation into the Light. Once you have placed a problem or concern into the Light, you can let it go, knowing that the Light is with it and that it is out of your hands. (If the situation later comes back to mind and distracts you, you can again place it into the Light.)

When you have finished placing people and situations in the Light, you can end your prayer with the following words: *I ask all of this in love, and I give my thanks.*

Sending the Light for the highest good to a person or situation—even a country—can be a great service. If you're concerned with problems in the Middle East, for example, instead of lamenting how terrible the situation is, you can do something practical by sending the Light: "For the highest good, I ask for the Light to be sent to the Middle East." In effect, sending the Light is making a choice to use your own divine nature to assist.

How, you may ask, do we know if sending the Light helps or not? The only answer is practical experience. Prayer can work even when the person prayed for is unaware of it. In a situation as complex as the conflict in the Middle East, it might be difficult to see results directly, but that does not mean that nothing is happening. As you use the Light more and more in your life, you will begin to notice changes, and you will have your own experience to draw on.

SPECIAL SELECTIONS
of RESOURCE *&* STUDY MATERIALS
by JOHN-ROGER, D.S.S.

The following materials can support you in learning more about the ideas presented in What's It Like Being You. *They can be ordered through the Movement of Spiritual Inner Awareness at: (800) 899-2665, www.msia.org, order@msia.org.*

Momentum: Letting Love Lead
Simple Practices for Spiritual Living
(with Paul Kaye, D.S.S.)

As much as we might like to have the important areas of our lives—Relationships, Health, Finances, and Career all settled and humming along, the reality for most of us is that there is always something out of balance, often causing stress and distress.

Rather than resisting or regretting imbalance, this book shows that there is an inherent wisdom in imbalance. Where there is imbalance, there is movement, and that movement "gives rise to a dynamic, engaging life that is full of learning, creativity, and growth." We can discover—in the very areas where we experience most of our problems and challenges—the greatest movement and the greatest opportunity for change.

The approach is not to try harder at making life work. Life already works. The big key is to bring loving into it. This book is about being loving in the moment. It is a course in loving.

Hardbound book #1893020185, $19.95

When Are You Coming Home?
A Personal Guide to Soul Transcendence
(with Pauli Sanderson, D.S.S.)

An intimate account of spiritual awakening that contains the elements of an adventure story. How did John-Roger attain the awareness of who he truly is? He approached life like a scientist in a laboratory. He found methods for integrating the sacred with the mundane, the practical with the mystical. He noted what worked and what didn't. Along with some fascinating stories, you will find in this book many practical keys for making your own life work better, for attuning to the source of wisdom that is always within you, and for making every day propel you further on your exciting adventure home.

Hardbound book #189302023, $19.95

Spiritual Warrior: The Art of Spiritual Living

Full of wisdom, humor, common sense, and hands-on tools for spiritual living, this book offers practical tips to take charge of our lives and create greater health, happiness, abundance, and loving. Becoming a spiritual warrior has nothing to do with violence. It is about using the positive qualities of the spiritual warrior—intention, ruthlessness, and impeccability—to counter negative personal habits and destructive relationships, especially when you are confronted with great adversity.

Hardbound book #01482936X, $20

Are You Available to Yourself?

Health, wealth, happiness, abundance, and riches are our heritage in this life. John-Roger reminds us that everything is available to us if we are available to ourselves and the spiritual life-force within us all.

Audiotape #7238, $10, Videotape #VC-7238, $20

Forgiveness: The Key to the Kingdom

Forgiveness is the key factor in personal liberation and spiritual progression. This book presents profound insights into forgiveness and the resulting personal joy and freedom. God's business is forgiving. This book provides encouragement and techniques for making it our business as well.

Softbound Book #0914829629, $12.95

Psychic Protection

In this book, John-Roger describes some of the invisible levels: the power of thoughts, the unconscious, elemental energies, and magic. More important, he discusses how to protect yourself against negativity that can be part of those levels. As you practice the simple techniques in this book, you can create a greater sense of well-being in and around you.

Softbound Book #0914829696, $6.95

Observation, The Key to Letting Go

In order to accept what is, we need to observe, like a scientist. "Observation," John-Roger says, "is the key to letting go and letting God." In observation, we are not getting involved with our emotions or bringing preconceived assumptions to the situation. Learning how to practice these principles more effectively can have tangible and profound benefits for bringing greater balance and happiness into our lives.

Audiotape #1552, $10

Success from the Inside Out

If you work hard, pay taxes, live "right," and still don't have what you want, this tape packet may be just the thing for you. Within the information it provides is a useful blueprint for discovering your innate abundance and your ability to create the life you dream of and deserve.

In this packet:
  Discover the eight essential steps to success
  Learn the magic of attitude and gratitude
  Awaken to greater opportunity and creativity
  Utilize your inner power of focus, thoughts, and words
  Experience a meditation for creating wealth
4-Audiotape packet #3913, $24.95

Turning Points to Personal Liberation

John-Roger presents direct, insightful information outlining the causes and cures of hurt, anger, confusion, jealousy, feelings of separation and loneliness, and other limiting behaviors and beliefs that often block our happiness, success, and enjoyment. These tapes contain practical keys and wisdom for gaining greater acceptance, understanding, loving, freedom, and liberation:

Keys to handling negative emotions
  Turning hurt and anger to acceptance and loving
  Five characteristics and cures of emotional mood swings
  Ten of life's essential questions
  Insecurity and what to do about it
  Healing the hurt
6-Audiotape packet, #0914829610, $45

Inner Worlds of Meditation

In this self-help guide to meditation, meditation practices are transformed into valuable and practical resources for exploring the spiritual realms and dealing with life more effectively. Included are a variety of meditations that can be used for gaining spiritual awareness, achieving greater relaxation, balancing the emotions, and increasing energy.

Softbound Book #0914829459, $11.95
6-Audiotape packet #0914829688, $45
3-CD packet #0914829645, $45

Health From the Inside Out

This packet of three audiotapes outlines how to use the energy of the body to create better health. Included are insights into the cycle of overeating and practical methods for overcoming it. There is a description of how to use the power of thought for better health, as well as to connect with the Supreme Source to promote greater healing and vitality. These tapes also describe how we sometimes promote "dis-ease" and how to change those patterns to gain better physical balance.

Topics on the tapes include:

> *Adapting toward health or adopting dis-ease*
> *Are you stuffing your expression?*
> *Are you unconsciously depleting your energy?*
> *Awakening beyond body consciousness*
> *Body balance meditation*

3-Audiotape packet #0914829327, $24.95

Soul Awareness Discourses
A Course in Soul Transcendence

Soul Awareness Discourses are designed to teach Soul Transcendence, which is becoming aware of yourself as a Soul and as one with God, not as a theory, but as a living reality. They are for people who want a consistent, time-proven approach to their spiritual enfoldment.

A set of Soul Awareness Discourses consists of 12 booklets, one to study and contemplate each month of the year. As you read each Discourse, you can activate an awareness of your Divine essence and deepen your relationship with God.

Spiritual in essence, Discourses are compatible with religious beliefs you might hold. In fact, most people find that Discourses support the experience of whatever path, philosophy, or religion (if any) they choose to follow. Simply put, Discourses are about eternal truths and the wisdom of the heart.

The first year of Discourses addresses topics ranging from creating success in the world to working hand-in-hand with Spirit.

INTRODUCTORY OFFER

A yearly set of Discourses is regularly $100. MSIA is offering the first year of Discourses at an introductory price of $50. Discourses come with a full, no-questions-asked, money-back guarantee. If at any time you decide this course of study is not right for you, simply return it, and you will promptly receive a full refund.

To order Discourses, email order@msia.org
or call 1-800-899-2665.

ABOUT THE AUTHORS

John-Roger, D.S.S.

A teacher and lecturer of international stature, John-Roger is an inspiration in the lives of many people around the world. For over four decades, his wisdom, humor, common sense, and love have helped people to discover the Spirit within themselves and find health, peace, and prosperity.

With two co-authored books on the *New York Times* Bestseller list to his credit, and more than four dozen spiritual and self-help books and audio albums, John-Roger offers extraordinary insights on a wide range of topics. He is the founder of the Church of the Movement of Spiritual Inner Awareness (MSIA), which focuses on Soul Transcendence; founder and Chancellor of the University of Santa Monica; founder and President of Peace Theological Seminary & College of Philosophy; founder of Insight Seminars; and founder and President of The Institute for Individual & World Peace.

John-Roger has given over 5,000 lectures and seminars worldwide, many of which are televised nationally on his cable program, "That Which Is," through the Network of Wisdoms. He has been a featured guest on "Larry King Live," "Politically Incorrect," "The Roseanne Show," and appears regularly on radio and television.

An educator and minister by profession, John-Roger continues to transform lives by educating people in the wisdom of the spiritual heart.

For more information about John-Roger, you may also want to visit: www.john-roger.org

Paul Kaye, D.S.S.

Paul Kaye has been a dedicated student of spiritual thought and practices since his youth in England. His explorations have taken him into Yoga, Zen, and the spiritual foundations of movement and the martial arts.

Paul's interests include the philosophies of such poets and teachers as Lao Tzu, Rumi, and Kabir and the esoteric teachings of Jesus Christ. Paul has designed workshops on the practical application of spiritual principles and presented them worldwide. Paul is a unique and remarkable presence. He brings an abundance of lightheartedness into whatever he does, and his presentations are inspiring, practical, and filled with a wonderful sense of humor and wisdom.

For over 30 years, he has studied with renowned educator and author John-Roger, and he is president of the Church of the Movement of Spiritual Inner Awareness (MSIA), an ecumenical, non-denominational church. Paul is an ordained minister and has a Doctorate in Spiritual Science.

FOR AUTHOR INTERVIEWS
& SPEAKING ENGAGEMENTS

Please contact Angel Gibson at:

Mandeville Press
3500 West Adams blvd.
Los Angeles, CA 90018
323-737-4055 (x155)
angel@mandevillepress.org

We welcome your comments and questions.

Mandeville Press
P.O. Box 513935
Los Angeles, CA 90051-1935
323-737-4055
jrbooks@mandevillepress.org
www.mandevillepress.org